Unleash Your Inner Champion

Odell Theadford

Published by Odell Theadford, 2024.

UNLEASH YOUR INNER CHAMPION

First edition. April 8, 2024.

Copyright © 2024 Odell Theadford.

ISBN: 979-8224550234

Written by Odell Theadford.

Also by Odell Theadford

A Jaz Blackwell Mystery
Sins of the Father

Standalone
Unleash Your Inner Champion

Watch for more at https://odelltheadford.org/.

1

EMBARKING ON A JOURNEY TO EXCELLENCE

In the realm of sports, there exists a path that courageous individuals follow to achieve greatness. It is a path that the weak-hearted do not tread as it requires unwavering determination, disciplined training, and a profound love for their sport. This transformative journey towards excellence does not only shape the physical abilities of an athlete but also molds their character, resilience, and ability to inspire others.

At its core, this journey is deeply personal – a voyage of self-discovery that lays the foundation for growth and self-realization. Getting to know oneself becomes the stride on this path to greatness. It involves introspection and self-reflection to identify one's strengths, weaknesses, and areas for improvement. A deep understanding of one's mind and motivations sets the stage for channeling passion into a source of motivation and perseverance.

Embarking on this quest for accomplishments demands relentless effort and unwavering dedication. There are no shortcuts that lead directly to success. It requires hours of practice aimed at pushing boundaries previously thought unattainable. The aspiring athlete must embody discipline, commitment, and an unyielding willingness to overcome obstacles, in the face of adversity or setbacks.

It is during times of challenge that a person's true character is revealed and their resilience begins to grow.

While physical ability plays a role in achieving excellence it is just one piece of the puzzle. Developing strength and emotional intelligence is equally important. An athlete's ability to navigate the difficulties of competition and stay focused and composed under pressure or after experiencing defeat sets them apart from ordinary athletes. It is in these moments that an athlete's true nature emerges, and their growth potential becomes evident.

The mindset adopted throughout this journey forms the foundation on which an athlete's success is built. Embracing a growth mindset believing that skills can be continuously developed and enhanced through effort and dedication becomes the driving force behind progress. Having an attitude rooted in self-belief propels athletes beyond self-doubt and perceived limitations.

However, achieving excellence does not happen alone. It requires having a network consisting of coaches, mentors, teammates and loved ones who provide guidance along the way.

These pillars of support offer guidance, accountability, and unwavering encouragement to push athletes towards achievements and provide comfort during tough times. Creating an environment that fosters champions is crucial in establishing a culture where excellence is the norm.

To reach greatness it is vital to optimize training and prioritize nutrition. The athlete's body serves as the instrument for accomplishments. Ensuring rest, proactive injury prevention, and rehabilitation enables the body to perform at its best. This holistic approach to wellness forms the foundation for excellence.

Simultaneously embracing a culture of learning and growth is important. Seeking wisdom from experts in the field studying the techniques of figures who have paved the way before them and staying up to date with advances in sports science propels athletes beyond complacency. It allows them to refine their strategies and remain at the forefront of their sport.

There exists an opportunity to inspire others within their sphere of influence and make an impact.

This transformative journey is much more than winning medals or achieving personal bests. It holds a significance that extends beyond the individual. Athletes possess the power to inspire others ignite their dreams and shape their communities. This expedition catalyzes transformation driving change and highlights the limitless potential of the human spirit.

As you embark on your pursuit of excellence remember that it is not only about reaching your destination but also about embracing the transformative power of the journey itself. It presents an opportunity for growth where you can break through self-imposed limitations and emerge as a more resilient and extraordinary version of yourself than you ever thought possible. Your path to greatness lies ahead—get ready to push your boundaries unlock untapped potential and fulfill your destiny as a champion. The adventure starts now.

2

IMMERSE YOURSELF IN THE PROCESS

When aiming for excellence it is essential to shift our focus from obsessing over results to fully immersing ourselves in the journey itself. Often athletes get too focused on the result – winning, setting records, or receiving recognition – that they lose sight of what matters, the journey of growth and improvement.

When we immerse ourselves in the journey our attention shifts to the moment. We fully engage in every practice session every workout and every competition dedicating our energy and focus to the here and now. We allow ourselves to completely embrace the experience embracing both challenges and opportunities for growth.

By shifting our focus from the outcome to the process itself we foster a mindset of learning and development. We realize that each step we take, each effort we make, contributes to our progress. We start appreciating triumphs along the way celebrating milestones and breakthroughs that arise from practice and perseverance.

This change in perspective enables us to establish a sense of understanding and connection with our chosen sport or athletic pursuit. We learn to appreciate its intricacies and subtleties recognizing that true mastery is not solely measured by accomplishments but, by internal transformation happening within us.

As we fully immerse ourselves in the process we cultivate a level of self-awareness. We begin to understand our strengths, weaknesses, and areas where we can improve with clarity. This self-awareness leads us to approach our training purposefully as we actively seek opportunities for growth and challenge ourselves to push beyond our limits.

Immersing ourselves in the journey fosters a sense of motivation. Instead of relying on external rewards or acknowledgment, we find satisfaction in the pursuit of mastery itself. We discover the delight and fulfillment that come from dedicating ourselves to celebrating the small victories and the progress we make daily.

As we fully embrace the process we also learn the significance of patience and persistence. We recognize that true excellence is not achieved overnight; it is a culmination of hours of practice and unwavering dedication to improvement. We value consistency. Show up every day embracing both the highs and lows that come with any journey.

Fully immersing ourselves in the process also empowers us to overcome adversity and setbacks. It instills within us resilience and determination that allows us to bounce back from failures and continue pursuing our goals. Not letting defeat define us we rise stronger and more determined knowing that setbacks serve as stepping-stones toward future success.

Immersing ourselves in the process leads us to a path of self-discovery. It enables us to unlock our potential by fully utilizing our abilities. We uncover strengths and push past the limitations we impose on ourselves. Our sport turns out to be a means of expressing our creativity and finding ways to highlight who we are.

As we delve deeper into this journey we develop mindfulness and an awareness of the moment. We begin to appreciate the beauty in each movement, every breath, and every sensation that our body experiences. Our connection with our sport deepens as we become attuned to its intricacies and complexities gaining an insight into its essence.

Beyond growth, immersing ourselves in this process also strengthens our bonds with others, we create a network of coaches, teammates, and fellow athletes who understand and value the importance of this journey. Together we share experiences, exchange knowledge, and support each other through both triumphs and challenges. This creates a sense of camaraderie that fuels our motivation.

Ultimately immersing ourselves in the process liberates us from seeking validation or conforming to expectations. It allows us to redefine success based on growth and self-improvement. We can reach a point where we no longer rely on others for validation. Instead, we find satisfaction in knowing that we have given our best efforts regardless of the result.

So, let go of the fixation on outcomes. Embrace the journey itself engage in the moment and witness how your pursuit of athletic excellence unfolds with more joy, resilience, and fulfillment. Believe in the power of this process. Embrace the continuous growth it offers. Always remember that true rewards lie within the journey itself.

3

CHAMPIONS ARE MADE IN THE MOMENTS

WHEN THE WORLD IS NOT WATCHING

In the depths of being alone where time seems to stand still and the outside world fades away exists a place called introspection. It is a realm where the quiet whispers of our thoughts become echoes and endless possibilities stretch out before us. It is in this realm that brave souls find comfort nurturing their hidden potential until it becomes a force.

As they embrace solitude these brave souls face a storm of emotions. Within the confines of their minds, they confront their fears, doubts, and vulnerabilities that could hinder their journey towards greatness. They understand that conquering these demons is crucial to building a foundation for their path to success.

In this space these courageous individuals navigate through the corridors of their past. They carefully examine memories and experiences with self-reflection in mind. They analyze their failures to learn lessons in humility and resilience. They also reignite past triumphs to draw strength and inspiration from those moments when they overcame challenges.

During these moments of solitude champions embrace silence as a cocoon for transformation.

They shed the layers of self-imposed limitations peeling away the doubts and insecurities that have wrapped around their spirit. They delve into the depths of their desires giving birth to goals that are even more ambitious and remarkable than before. They marvel at the potential that resides within them waiting to be unleashed upon the world.

Immersing themselves in this timeless realm champions weave dreams and aspirations like threads into the fabric of their lives. They bring forth visions that gleam with a clarity only discovered in moments of solitude. With every stroke of their imagination, they create depictions of a future where greatness is their inherent right.

Within this solitude champions embrace their vulnerabilities and authenticity it brings. They understand that true strength lies not in invincibility but in having the courage to expose weaknesses and imperfections. They cultivate compassion and empathy within themselves recognizing that forging connections with others holds power for impact and transformation.

While the world remains unaware of the symphony of their growth champions persistently labor on. They refine their skills honing their expertise with a commitment to excellence. They commit themselves to ending the pursuit of knowledge and personal growth by recognizing that true expertise comes from a desire to improve.

In the peacefulness of solitude champions embark on a journey delving into their subconscious to uncover the essence of who they are. They explore their beliefs and values that shape how they see the world. They discover the passions that ignite their spirits and the purpose that drives them forward. With unwavering clarity, they align their actions with their aspirations forging a path for themselves.

While the world remains unaware of their transformation, champions persist. They endure sleepless nights, setbacks, and sacrifices along their journey. With a thirst for greatness that goes beyond external recognition they persevere.

Deep within, champions tap into a wellspring of resilience flowing through their veins. They summon this strength to navigate storms and overcome obstacles in their path. They learn that setbacks are not failures but opportunities to refine their approach and emerge even stronger.

In the depths of solitude lies self-discovery for champions. They find their voice, purpose, and personal power.

They emerge from the cocoon of self-reflection spreading their wings wide and ready to reach new heights. With a sense of confidence and determination they step into the world carrying the light of their greatness to illuminate a path for others.

So, my dear friend, delve into the depths of solitude. Embrace the power that lies within. Allow silence to be your guide as you embark on a journey of self-discovery. In this realm nurture the seeds of passion, perseverance, and strength until they blossom into a symphony of achievements. When the world eventually turns its attention toward you they will witness a champion who has triumphed over silent struggles and emerged victorious for all to behold.

4

SHOW UP AND WORK HARD EVERY DAY

YOUR EFFORT IS THE FOUNDATION

In the realm of champions there is no substitute for work and unwavering dedication. Natural talent alone or relying on luck will not cut it. True winners understand that success is constructed upon the foundation of effort day after day.

Taking the initiative and showing up is the first step. It means committing yourself to your aspirations and goals. It means refusing to make excuses or allowing distractions to hinder your progress. When you show up you send a message to both yourself and the world that you are dead serious about your ambitions.

Merely showing up is just part of the equation. Once you have arrived it is essential to be prepared to give it your all. Hard work acts as the driving force that propels you forward and pushes you beyond your limits. It is the ingredient that transforms dreams into reality.

The level of effort you put in truly reflects your level of commitment. It is the distinguishing factor that separates those who settle for average from those who strive for greater heights. Embracing the grind, enduring hours work, and tackling difficult challenges are what distinguish champions from others. These moments when nobody is watching are when true character is forged, and resilience built.

Your effort should never falter based on circumstances. Whether you are feeling exhausted, lacking motivation, or confronted with obstacles it is essential to persevere and keep moving. It is during these times that your genuine character shines through and your potential becomes evident.

What does it truly mean to work? It means getting up even when you are tempted to hit the snooze button. It means staying up putting in hours even when others have already called it a day. It means sacrificing leisure time and temporary pleasures for long term fulfillment.

Hard work isn't about exertion; it requires mental strength. It entails overcoming self-doubt quieting that critic and persevering in the face of adversity. It is about directing your energy and focus on tasks and projects that align with your goals.

Furthermore, hard work isn't an endeavor. It involves surrounding yourself with individuals who share your drive and ambition. Whether they are mentors, coaches or teammates having a support system of inspiring people who hold you accountable can make all the difference.

On the journey towards achieving greatness there will inevitably be failures and setbacks. Nobody is immune to disappointment. However, it is in these moments that true champions emerge. They gain knowledge from their mistakes adapt their approach and continue moving. Failure is not the end. It serves as a stepping-stone towards achieving success.

True success is not solely measured by achievements. It encompasses development, learning, and self-improvement. The process of work and devotion molds your character sharpens your skills and fosters resilience. It is a journey that extends beyond the outcome.

The path to success is not always glamorous. It often entails challenges, sacrifices, and uncertainties. Remember, the more effort you put in the more fortunate you become. Champions are not merely lucky; they have earned their success through unwavering dedication and an unyielding commitment to their craft.

By exerting effort, you become the architect of your destiny. You seize control of your life. Transform your dreams into reality. The ability to bring about change lies in your hands. It is through daily endeavors that you shape your future.

Each day presents an opportunity to reaffirm your dedication and push yourself further ahead. Embrace the discomfort. Stretch your boundaries because it is during those moments that growth transpires. The journey ahead might be lengthy. But it is worth embarking on.

As you set foot on this path always remember that hard work is not a burden, rather it's a privilege. It is truly a privilege to have the chance to pursue your passions and commit yourself to something. Treasure the process. Find joy in your progress because it is the journey itself that brings fulfillment.

In the pursuit of greatness there will be moments of uncertainty and weariness. Times when you question if all your efforts are worthwhile. During those moments look back at how far you have come. Reflect on the obstacles you have conquered and the small victories that have shaped your path. Recall why you started and let that spark within you keep pushing you.

So, when your alarm clock rings in the morning, or when doubts begin to creep in, or when obstacles appear insurmountable remind yourself why you embarked on this journey. Embrace the grind, welcome sweat and discomfort. By showing up every day with dedication and working hard you are laying down the groundwork for a life of fulfilment.

Your present efforts will become tomorrow's legacy. The world may not immediately notice your commitment. Over time as part of life's tapestry, your hard work will be acknowledged and celebrated.

Be present put in the effort and allow your deeds to make an impact rather than your words. You have the power to shape your future as a writer with the pen firmly in your grasp.

5

PAY ATTENTION TO THE DETAILS THEY MATTER MORE THAN YOU THINK

When striving for greatness it is often the little things that can have the greatest impact. Although it may seem tiresome or unnecessary, paying attention to the details is crucial in attaining success.

By focusing on these specifics, we can refine our work and ensure its quality. It is within these nuances that true excellence resides. Whether you are an athlete, an artist, or a professional in the business world these details can improve your performance.

Imagine a musician playing a melody. The notes flow effortlessly captivating the audience. However, what if the musician neglects to tune their instrument? Suddenly harmony is lost. That magical connection with the audience dissipates. It is the attention to detail that elevates a performance into a masterpiece.

Similarly, athletes comprehend the significance of concentrating on the details. A slight adjustment in their technique or form can result in shaving off seconds from their race time. By analyzing every aspect of their performance, they uncover areas for improvement and push themselves beyond limits.

Success in the business world heavily relies on paying attention to details. The ability to present a crafted proposal, proofread reports diligently, or plan presentations meticulously often determines triumph. These elements are essential for establishing credibility and leaving a lasting impression on clients or colleagues. They showcase professionalism and a commitment to delivering the work.

Being attentive to the specifics is not about delivering results; it also signifies a strong dedication to learning and personal growth. It is through this attention that we uncover insights and explore new opportunities. When we fully immerse ourselves in our work we can notice the intricacies that might otherwise go unnoticed.

Focusing on the particulars fosters presence. This mindset allows us to wholeheartedly engage with our tasks without merely going through the motions. It is about being fully present in the moment and truly connected with our work. By paying attention to details we tap into a wellspring of creativity and resourcefulness that allows us to exceed our own expectations.

Paying attention to details also extends to how we interact with others. It involves listening, observing body language, and discerning cues in communication. These nuances can convey messages and help us better understand the needs and aspirations of those around us. By attending to these details in our relationships we cultivate empathy, build trust, and forge meaningful connections.

In a world where speed and efficiency often take precedence it can be tempting to overlook the significance of paying attention to the finer points. Dedicating time and effort to focusing on the small things sets us apart from our competition. It demonstrates professionalism and excellence in our fields.

By immersing ourselves in our work we can uncover solutions and push the boundaries of what was previously believed to be achievable. Attention to detail enables us to identify areas for improvement allowing us to continuously refine our skills and surpass our expectations.

In every undertaking considering the intricacies does not only enhance the outcome but also provides a deep sense of fulfillment. When we know that we have invested effort into every aspect and left no stone unturned we can take pride in our accomplishments. This feeling of satisfaction fuels our motivation and propels us along our path.

Paying attention to details is not merely a task but rather an art form in itself. It demands discipline, concentration, and perseverance. This commitment exemplifies dedication and an unwavering pursuit of excellence.

As you begin your path, to success it is crucial to focus on the small things. Embrace the importance of being meticulous in your pursuit of excellence. Take pride in the precision that distinguishes your work. "By paying attention to the details you can enhance your performance, accomplish remarkable feats, and truly make a meaningful difference. Developing habits that foster greatness is the key element."

6

GET ENOUGH SLEEP TO ALLOW YOUR BODY TO REFRESH AND REBUILD

Enough sleep is often ignored but essential for allowing your body to recharge and repair itself. It can be tempting in today's fast-paced world to give up on sleep to have more time for work or leisure activities. However, through this we fail to realize how crucial it is to our general health and performance.

Sleep is not just about resting, it is a process that helps in the repairing of the physical body and the mind. During sleep, many rejuvenating processes occur within our bodies including muscle growth and repair, tissue regeneration as well as hormonal regulation. Without these processes, optimal physical function cannot be sustained resulting from exhaustive tasks.

During sleep, growth hormones are released by our bodies which plays a critical role in muscle repair and growth. This hormone helps restore damaged muscle tissues, fortify joints, and boost overall bodily strength. Reduced athletic performance, higher chances of injuries occurrence, and delayed recovery periods are some effects of inadequate sleep interfering with these processes.

Moreover, there is a tight bond between sleep and cognitive ability as well as mental health. It consolidates memories, boosts creative skill and enhances concentration level so that good decisions can be made. Conversely, poor sleeping pattern hampers cognitive actions while having low moods plus intensifying conditions such as anxiety or depression.

To get enough sleep necessary for refreshing and rebuilding your body it becomes very important that you prioritize it among your daily routine practices. Some additional tips for quality sleep are:

1) Set up a regular sleeping timetable: Aim at going to bed at the same time every day coupled with waking up at the same hour so that your body's internal clock may adjust accordingly. Consistency contributes towards better quality of your night's rest and its length too. When you have a specific time when your body knows that it will receive rest it prepares itself thus making falling asleep possible easily.

2) Make sure your bedroom is conducive for sleep: Darkness, silence and the right temperature must dominate in your sleeping place. These conditions make sure that you have the best sleep ever by preventing all external disruptions. The blackout curtains, ear plugs. or white noise machines help to create a calming atmosphere that aids in relaxation and sleep. Additionally, purchasing an appropriate mattress and pillows can increase comfort and improve the quality of sleep.

3) Relaxation techniques must be applied: Some activities like reading a book, taking a warm bath, or meditating before bed can help you relax. Such activities calm your mind and body in preparation for deep sleep. Engaging in these calming activities helps the body to gradually shift from the day's tensions to tranquility that enables better sleeping conditions. Alternatively other techniques such as deep breathing exercises or progressive muscle relaxation may work just as well.

4) Caffeine and alcohol intake limitation: Stay away from stimulants like caffeine or alcohol shortly before bed because they can interfere with one's sleeping patterns thus denying you restful sleep. Caffeine prevents you from sleeping by stopping hormones responsible for causes of sleep in the brain while alcohol might cause drowsiness at first, but it disrupts regular sleep cycle resulting in less restful slumber. Instead, it is recommended to take herbal tea or warm milk drinks before bed.

5) Exercise regularly: Consistent physical activity may enhance sleep quality, but avoid vigorous exercise a few hours before bed, as it may stimulate your body and make it difficult for you to fall asleep. Regular exercise during the day contributes to better sleep because it helps in controlling your body's circadian rhythm and uses up excess energy. Moreover, outdoor activities can improve your exposure to natural light which regulates sleep-wake patterns.

6) Practice good sleep hygiene: Create a bedtime routine that includes activities like dimming lights, listening to soft music, and avoiding stimulating electronics before going to bed. These devices such as smartphones and tablets emit blue light that inhibits melatonin production hence making it harder for one to sleep. Thus, switching off screens an hour before going to bed is a natural way of relaxing your body so that the mind knows that it is time to sleep rather than using them in place of reading physical books or just practicing a calming hobby.

When you prioritize sleep allowing enough time for your body to recover and repair itself properly, this will lead to increased physical performance, improved mental clarity, and overall well-being. Let us not forget that rested bodies perform better under pressure; they can withstand intense training sessions with ease thus leading us closer towards our goals in life. By doing so you will realize how powerful sleeping is and most importantly why it should not be viewed as a luxury but rather a necessity towards having good health full of satisfaction.

7

SWEAT TODAY, SMILE TOMORROW

In life, there are no shortcuts to success. It requires dedication, perseverance, and hard work. It is a journey of self-discovery and growth, filled with ups and downs, challenges, and triumphs. One must be willing to put in the effort and sweat today to reap the rewards and smile tomorrow.

Sweating today goes beyond the physical act of perspiration. It represents the essence of commitment and determination. It is about pushing oneself to the limits, testing boundaries, and surpassing expectations. It is understood that greatness is not handed on a silver platter but earned through persistence and resilience.

From the early morning hours to the deep of night, the path to success is paved with hours of hard work and sacrifice. It is waking up before the sun, while the world still lies in slumber, and immersing oneself in the pursuit of goals. It is utilizing every minute of the day, leaving no room for procrastination or excuses.

Yet, the sweat that drips from our brows is not solely a representation of physical exertion. It signifies the effort we pour into mastering our craft, the discipline we maintain to stay focused, and the mental strength we develop to overcome obstacles. It is the sweat of determination, perseverance, and passion, interwoven into the fabric of our lives.

Sweating today is not limited to a specific domain or field. It applies to every aspect of life. Whether it is pursuing a career, mastering a skill, building meaningful relationships, or striving for personal growth, success demands sweat. It demands sacrifices, late nights, and early mornings. It calls for the courage to step out of the comfort zone and embrace the unknown.

Within the realm of career pursuits, sweating today might involve acquiring new knowledge and skills to remain at the forefront of one's industry. It might mean taking on challenging projects that stretch our abilities and demand our full dedication. It could even require making difficult decisions and sacrifices, such as leaving behind the familiar to pursue opportunities that align with our passions and aspirations.

In the realm of personal growth, sweating today is about facing our fears and examining our shortcomings. It is acknowledged that growth comes from stepping outside our comfort zones, taking risks, and embracing uncertainty. Sweat becomes the currency exchanged for self-reflection, self-improvement, and the expansion of our capabilities.

Sweating today is also about overcoming obstacles and setbacks. It means acknowledging that failure is an inevitable part of the journey. It is about learning from mistakes, adapting, and moving forward. It is having the resilience to get up after every fall, to dust off the dirt, and to keep pushing towards the finish line.

Furthermore, it is essential to recognize that success is not a solitary endeavor but a collaborative effort. Sweating today involves surrounding oneself with like-minded individuals who share the same drive and determination. These comrades-in-sweat become sources of inspiration, encouragement, and support in times of difficulty. Together, they fuel each other's ambitions and create an environment where everyone can thrive.

But amidst the hard work and sweat, it is crucial to remember the significance of balance. While the pursuit of success demands dedication, it is equally important to take care of our physical and mental well-being. Rest and recovery are essential to maintain peak performance and prevent burnout. It is about finding harmony between pushing ourselves and practicing self-care.

And when tomorrow comes, and we look back on the sweat we have shed, we will smile. We will smile not only because of the achievements and milestones we have reached but also because of the growth and transformation we have undergone. We will smile because the challenges we face have shaped us into stronger, more resilient individuals.

The smile tomorrow is not just about external validation or tangible success. It is about the satisfaction of knowing we have given our best. It is about the confidence that comes from knowing we have pursued our dreams with unwavering dedication. It is about the joy of embracing the journey, relishing both the highs and lows, and recognizing the beauty in the process.

Let us remember that success is not a destination but a lifelong pursuit. It is a continuous journey marked by sweat, challenges, and growth. So, let us embrace the sweat today and smile tomorrow, for it is in the sweat that we discover our true strength and in the smile that we find fulfillment and happiness.

8

UNLEASH YOUR INNER CHAMPION

YOUR ONLY LIMIT IS YOU

Our lives are shaped by the limits we impose on ourselves. These limits take various forms, whether it is fear of failure, doubt of our abilities, or the belief that we are not deserving of success. We become accustomed to living within these boundaries, believing they are our reality and accepting them as our fate.

Yet, if we dare to challenge these self-imposed limits, we can unlock a world of infinite possibilities. We must understand that the power lies within each of us to redefine what is possible and push beyond our perceived boundaries.

To begin this transformative journey, we must first take an honest and introspective look at the limits we have created. Are they truly rooted in reality or are they a result of our thoughts and beliefs? Often, we discover that these limits are mere illusions, constructs of our minds that hold us back from fully embracing our potential.

Fear, a pervasive and often paralyzing limit is one that many of us regularly face. Fear of the unknown, fear of failure, and fear of rejection can loom over us, preventing us from taking risks and pursuing our dreams. However, what if we were to reframe fear as a catalyst for growth? What if we saw fear as a sign that we are on the brink of something extraordinary? By acknowledging our fears and moving forward despite them, we unlock opportunities for personal growth and transformation. We must embrace fear as an ally, a guiding force that prompts us to step outside our comfort zone and discover the magnificent possibilities that lie just beyond.

Another limit we frequently encounter is self-doubt. We question our abilities, comparing ourselves to others and believing we fall short. This unwavering belief in our inadequacy becomes a self-fulfilling prophecy, hindering our progress and stifling our creativity. However, when we shift our focus from comparing and competing to learning and growing, we realize that everyone has a unique journey and timeline. Our worth is not determined by external validation but by the dedication and resilience we bring to our endeavors. By nurturing self-compassion and cultivating self-belief, we begin to dismantle the walls of self-doubt, paving the way for unrestrained personal growth and achievement.

The stories we tell ourselves also contribute to the limits we impose. Past failures or disappointments can leave us feeling trapped in a narrative of defeat. However, these setbacks are not permanent markers of our abilities, but rather stepping-stones towards success. By reframing our experiences as valuable lessons and opportunities for growth, we release ourselves from the constraints of our past and open ourselves up to a future filled with endless possibilities. We must acknowledge our achievements, no matter how small, and draw strength from them as we navigate the path toward greater success.

Overcoming self-imposed limits requires a commitment to personal development. It demands that we challenge our beliefs, question our assumptions, and cultivate a growth mindset. Surrounding ourselves with inspiring individuals and seeking out mentors who have defied conventional limits can provide us with the motivation and guidance we need to push beyond our preconceived boundaries. Reading books, attending seminars, and engaging in self-reflection become instrumental in reshaping our mindset and expanding our sense of what is truly possible.

But personal growth alone is not enough; we must also take relentless action. Dreams remain dreams unless we transform them into concrete goals and take tangible steps toward their realization.

It is through consistent effort, perseverance, and resilience that we break free from the chains of self-imposed limits and move closer to our aspirations. Failure becomes not an obstacle but an opportunity for learning and growth. Each setback propels us forward, fueling our determination to overcome, and allowing us to tap into our untapped potential.

Remember, our only limit is ourselves. As we shed the confines of fear, doubt, and negative narratives, we tap into our inherent capacity to embrace challenges, expand our capabilities, and soar to new heights. When we believe in our potential, release our limits, and take relentless action, the world becomes an expansive canvas where we can create our extraordinary masterpiece of success, fulfillment, and happiness. The journey to breaking free from self-imposed limits is not an easy one, but it is undeniably worth it – for in the pursuit of reaching our fullest potential, we discover that there are no limits to what we can achieve and become.

9

SUCCESS BEGINS WITH BELIEVING IN YOURSELF

In the pursuit of success, one of the most critical factors lies within oneself: the belief in one's abilities and potential. Without this firm belief, it becomes challenging to overcome obstacles, persist in the face of setbacks, and take the necessary risks to achieve greatness.

Believing in yourself is not a fleeting thought but a deep-rooted conviction that transcends external validation. It stems from recognizing your inherent worth and understanding that you possess unique talents and strengths that can be honed and utilized to achieve remarkable feats.

This unwavering belief in oneself acts as a foundation upon which you can build your success. It empowers you to take action, make bold decisions, and push past any self-doubt or negative thoughts that may arise. With each step forward, the belief in yourself resonates within your being, propelling you towards new heights.

Cultivating this belief requires self-reflection and a conscious effort to challenge limiting beliefs ingrained within us. Society often imposes predetermined notions of success, dictating what it should look like and how it should be achieved. It is easy to fall into the trap of comparison and self-doubt, feeling inadequate when measuring progress against others. To combat this, it is essential to redefine success on your terms, focusing on personal growth and fulfillment rather than external validation.

To develop a strong belief in yourself, start by acknowledging your strengths and accomplishments. Take stock of your past achievements, no matter how modest or insignificant they may seem. Recognize the inner strength and capabilities that allowed you to overcome challenges and taste success. Celebrate these victories, no matter how small, and use them as a constant reminder of your potential for greatness.

Surround yourself with positive and supportive individuals who believe in you and your abilities. Seek out mentors or role models who have achieved success in areas aligned with your goals. Their guidance, wisdom, and encouragement can help fuel your belief in yourself. Learning from their experiences and adopting their strategies can provide valuable insights and shortcuts on your journey.

Continuous self-improvement plays a crucial role in building and maintaining self-belief. Set challenging yet attainable goals that stretch your capabilities and invite growth. As you make progress and achieve milestones, your confidence in your abilities will naturally solidify. Embrace the inevitable mistakes and failures along the way as essential learning experiences, reframing them as bridges rather than setbacks.

Practicing self-care and self-compassion is paramount. Success is not an overnight phenomenon, but a journey that requires perseverance and resilience. Treat yourself with kindness and patience, nurturing a positive inner dialogue that reinforces your belief in yourself. Celebrate even the smallest victories and acknowledge the effort you put forth in every endeavor. Remember, self-belief is a journey, and each step forward is a testament to your commitment and dedication.

As you progress on your journey toward success, be aware that external validations may fluctuate. The belief in yourself must be steadfast and independent of external circumstances. Surroundings may change, opinions may vary, but your self-belief remains constant and unshakable.

It is important to cultivate a growth mindset. Embrace the idea that abilities and intelligence can be developed through dedication and hard work. Rather than seeing setbacks as failures, view them as valuable learning opportunities that add to your growth. This mindset allows you to approach challenges with resilience and adaptability, knowing that failure is not a permanent state but a temporary setback on the path to success.

Additionally, self-belief is not limited to individual efforts. Building a network of support and collaborating with like-minded individuals can greatly enhance your self-belief and overall success. Surround yourself with people who inspire and challenge you, who believe in your dreams, and who encourage you to reach for the stars. Share your aspirations and goals with trusted friends, mentors, and colleagues, allowing their support and feedback to fuel your belief in yourself.

Furthermore, developing a clear sense of purpose and aligning your actions with your values strengthens your belief in yourself. When your goals and actions are congruent with your core values, every step toward success feels more meaningful and gratifying. Understanding why you are pursuing a particular path and how it aligns with your overarching vision gives you the motivation and drive to persist, even when faced with obstacles.

It is important to cultivate a mindset of abundance rather than scarcity. Believe that opportunities are abundant, and that success is not limited to a select few. Celebrate the accomplishments of others, as their achievements do not diminish your potential for success. Embrace collaboration and the power of collective growth, knowing that there is enough success to go around.

In conclusion, success starts with believing in yourself. Embrace your unique qualities, trust in your abilities, and strive for excellence. Cultivate a deep-rooted conviction that transcends external validation, establishing an unbreakable foundation for your aspirations. With unwavering self-belief, you can confidently overcome obstacles, persist through challenges, and create the success you desire and deserve.

10

DREAMS DON'T WORK UNLESS YOU DO

In life, we all have dreams and aspirations. We envision a future where we have achieved our goals and are living our best lives. These dreams may be big or small, but they all have one thing in common: they require action.

Dreams are not realized by dreaming. They require dedication, hard work, and perseverance. It is not enough to simply imagine the life we want; we must actively pursue it.

Too often, people fall into the trap of thinking that dreams will magically come true without any effort on their part. They wait for opportunities to fall into their lap, hoping that success will come knocking on their door. But the truth is, that dreams require sweat, determination, and a whole lot of hustle.

If you want to turn your dreams into reality, you must be willing to put in the work. This means setting clear, achievable goals that align with your dreams. Break down your big dreams into smaller, manageable steps that you can take each day. With a solid plan in place, you will be able to navigate your way toward your dreams more effectively.

Taking consistent action is crucial. It is not enough to work hard for a day or two and then give up when you face challenges or setbacks. Dreams require endurance and the ability to persevere even when things get tough. Expect obstacles along the way; they are part of the journey. Embrace them as opportunities for growth and learning and keep pushing forward.

One of the keys to success is consistency. Building habits that support your dreams will help you stay on track even when motivation wavers. Create a routine that includes actions aligned with your goals and stick to it. Whether it is writing for a set amount of time each day, practicing a skill, or networking with like-minded individuals, consistency will help you make progress.

It is easy to get discouraged along the way. There will be times when it feels like you are not making any progress or when obstacles seem insurmountable. But these are the moments that separate the dreamers from the achievers. It is during these moments that you must dig deep, find your inner strength, and keep pushing forward.

It is important to surround yourself with the right support system. Seek out individuals who believe in your dreams and can provide encouragement and guidance. Surrounding yourself with like-minded people who have similar goals can be incredibly motivating and give you the inspiration you need to keep going.

Remember to celebrate even the smallest victories along the way. Acknowledge the progress you have made and the milestones you have reached. Celebrating these wins will fuel your motivation and remind you that you are on the right path.

Dreams do not work unless you do. They do not come true by chance or luck. They require your effort, your commitment, and your unwavering belief in yourself and your abilities.

So, do not just dream about the life you want. Act. Start today, right now. Break down your dreams into manageable steps and take one small action every day. Stay focused, stay motivated, and never lose sight of why you started in the first place.

The journey to realizing your dreams may be long, and the road may be filled with ups and downs, but in the end, it will all be worth it. The satisfaction of achieving your dreams, of knowing that you gave it your all, is unlike anything else.

Dreams are not for the passive; they are for the doers, the ones who are willing to put in the work. So, roll up your sleeves, get to work, and make your dreams a reality. Because in the end, it is not about the dreams you have; it is about the dreams you make come true.

11

PUSH YOURSELF BECAUSE NO ONE ELSE

IS GOING TO DO IT FOR YOU

In life, there are no guarantees that someone else will push you towards your goals and dreams. The responsibility falls on your shoulders to take charge and push yourself to achieve greatness. It may be tempting to rely on others for motivation and support, but ultimately, it is your determination and self-discipline that will determine your success.

Pushing yourself goes beyond physical exertion; it encompasses mental strength and resilience. It means setting high standards for yourself and consistently striving to exceed them. Pushing yourself requires discipline, dedication, and an unwavering belief in your abilities. It means challenging yourself to step out of your comfort zone and confront the unknown.

Often, fear of failure holds us back from pushing ourselves. We become comfortable with mediocrity, settling for what is safe and familiar. But growth and progress require us to venture into uncharted territory, to push the boundaries of what we believe is possible. It is in those uncomfortable moments that we discover our true potential and realize that success lies just beyond the walls of our comfort zone.

At times, you can feel exhausted and even isolated to be solely responsible for your own motivation and progress. It is human nature to crave external validation and support from others. We seek approval, recognition, and encouragement to fuel our determination. However, relying on others for your drive and determination can lead to disappointment. People's own priorities and goals may diverge from yours, and their support may waver or fade altogether. When that happens, it is crucial to have the internal fortitude to continue pushing forward.

There will be days when everything seems to be going against you, when obstacles seem insurmountable, and when giving up may appear to be the easiest option. It is during these moments that you must find the strength to push through. Remind yourself of your aspirations and the reasons why you started this journey in the first place. Stay focused on the end goal and visualize the satisfaction and fulfillment that comes with achieving it.

Pushing yourself also means taking responsibility for your own growth and development. Seek out opportunities for improvement and actively work on enhancing your skills and knowledge. Continuously educate yourself, whether through formal education, self-study, or seeking mentorship. Embrace challenges as opportunities for growth, and view failures as steps on the path to success. Learn from your mistakes, adapt your approach, and keep pushing forward.

Surrounding yourself with like-minded individuals who inspire and motivate you is essential. Seek out positive influencers, mentors, or friends who challenge you to be your best self. Engage in meaningful conversations and share ideas to expand your perspective. Collaborate with others who share your passion and drive, as their energy and dedication will provide invaluable support on your journey.

While external influences can provide guidance and inspiration, it is crucial not to rely solely on them. Ultimately, the decision to push yourself and create the life you desire lies within you. Cultivate a deep sense of self-awareness and introspection. Clarify your values, goals, and purpose. By aligning your actions with your authentic self, you can tap into an endless reservoir of inner strength and motivation.

Developing a growth mindset is an essential component of pushing yourself. Embrace challenges as opportunities for learning and growth. Approach obstacles with curiosity rather than fear, knowing that every difficulty carries a valuable lesson. View setbacks as temporary and resiliently bounce back, armed with newfound knowledge and determination.

Pushing yourself is not about creating unrealistic expectations or burning out from constant striving. It is a balanced pursuit of continual improvement and stepping outside of your comfort zone. Set achievable yet challenging goals that stretch your capabilities. Break these goals down into smaller milestones, allowing you to track your progress and celebrate each accomplishment along the way. By recognizing and appreciating the small victories, you fuel your motivation to keep pushing forward.

Remember, success is not linear, and setbacks are an inevitable part of the journey. Embrace the setbacks as opportunities to recalibrate, reassess, and realign your path. Acknowledge that stepping out of your comfort zone may bring discomfort, uncertainty, and even failure. However, it is through these experiences that you grow and evolve, ultimately becoming a stronger version of yourself.

When you push yourself, you gain a sense of empowerment and fulfillment that is truly unmatched. You begin to see that you can achieve more than you ever thought possible. Each step forward becomes a testament to your resilience and dedication. The journey towards pushing yourself may be challenging, but the rewards that come from surpassing your limits are immeasurable.

As you embark on this journey of self-motivation and relentless pursuit of your goals, remember to find joy in the process. Celebrate your progress, honor your efforts, and savor the small victories. Push yourself not out of a sense of obligation or pressure, but because deep within you, you know that you are capable of creating a life of purpose and greatness.

So, push yourself, believe in your abilities, seek support when needed, and let your inner strength guide you toward the extraordinary. Push yourself because no one else is going to do it for you.

12

WINNERS DON'T QUIT BECAUSE THEY KNOW QUITTING ISN'T AN OPTION

In life's journey, we are often faced with formidable challenges and daunting obstacles that test our perseverance and determination. These moments of adversity serve as litmus tests, separating the true winners from those who yield to defeat. Winners understand that quitting is not an option; it is an admission of defeat and a surrender of dreams. They push through the hardships, armed with an unwavering belief in their abilities and an unshakable determination to achieve their goals.

The path to success is rarely a straight, smooth road. It is a treacherous trail, laden with unpredictable twists and turns. Along this winding path, winners encounter setbacks, failures, and moments of self-doubt. These obstacles, rather than discouraging them, ignite a fire within, propelling them forward.

While others may falter and retreat when faced with defeat, winners use setbacks as lessons towards growth and improvement. They internalize their failures, seeking valuable lessons amidst the disappointment. Winners refuse to accept defeat as a permanent state; instead, they view it as a temporary detour, redirecting their journey towards success.

The resilience of winners shines brightest in the face of failure. They possess an intrinsic ability to rise above their setbacks, fueled by the learnings that only failure can offer. Failure becomes a catalyst for change, a moment of reflection and introspection that propels them towards greatness. It is in these humbling moments that winners uncover their true strength, pushing themselves to adapt, innovate, and refine their approach.

Furthermore, winners possess an unwavering commitment to their goals. They understand that success is not a quick fix; it is built upon a solid foundation of discipline, consistency, and unwavering dedication. Winners are willing to put in the hard work and make the necessary sacrifices, knowing that the rewards are not immediate but ultimately worth the effort.

A winner's mindset thrives on growth. They embrace challenges as opportunities for personal development, rather than viewing them as roadblocks to happiness. Winners constantly seek to expand their knowledge and skill sets, embracing the concept of lifelong learning. They step outside of their comfort zones, venturing into uncharted territories, and embracing the unknown. It is through these courageous leaps that winners discover new strengths and capabilities, transcending their previous limitations.

Truly successful individuals understand that perseverance is the key to victory. They possess an unyielding determination that propels them forward, even in the face of insurmountable odds. This unwavering resolve stems from an unwavering belief in oneself and the power of perseverance. Winners remain fiercely focused on their goals, irrespective of distractions or doubts, keeping their eyes firmly fixed on the finish line.

In the game of life, winners understand that success is not guaranteed. It is something that must be earned through relentless effort, resilience, and an unshakeable belief in oneself. They embrace the challenges, setbacks, and failures as part of the journey and use them as fuel to propel them towards their goals. Winners never quit, for they know that quitting only leads to regret and missed opportunities.

As we navigate the maze of life, let us remember that winners never quit, and quitters never win. Embrace the challenges, learn from failures, and persist with unwavering determination. Success awaits those who refuse to succumb to defeat, who are willing to push through the darkest moments and emerge stronger on the other side. In the pursuit of victory, remember that you, too, can be a winner, discovering the resilience, strength, and greatness that lie within you.

13

HARD WORK BEATS TALENT WHEN TALENT DOES NOT WORK HARD

In the realm of success, talent is often highly regarded and admired. People with natural abilities in a particular field are often seen as the ones destined for greatness. However, talent alone is not always enough to guarantee success. In fact, there is a saying that goes, "Hard work beats talent when talent doesn't work hard." This belief highlights the importance of dedication, perseverance, and determination in achieving one's goals.

While talent can provide an initial advantage, it is through hard work that individuals can truly unlock their full potential. Hard work involves putting in the time and effort to improve skills, overcome obstacles, and consistently pushing oneself beyond their comfort zone. It is the willingness to go the extra mile, to practice relentlessly, and to learn from failures that sets individuals apart.

One of the key aspects of hard work is consistency. It is not enough to work hard for a short period of time or sporadically. True success comes from a commitment to continual improvement and growth. It is in the daily grind, the hours of practice, and the dedication to learning that individuals can master their craft.

Hard work also builds character and resilience. The challenges and setbacks that come along the way serve as valuable lessons and opportunities for growth. When talent alone is relied upon without the work ethic to back it up, individuals can easily become complacent or give up when faced with obstacles. On the other hand, those who have developed a strong work ethic through discipline and hard work are better equipped to persevere, adapt, and ultimately succeed.

In many cases, individuals who may initially lack natural talent can surpass those who have been gifted with innate abilities simply because they are willing to put in more effort and work harder. It is through their relentless determination, drive, and commitment that they are able to bridge the gap and exceed expectations.

Moreover, hard work not only enhances talent but also helps discover hidden talents. Many people may possess hidden talents that remain undiscovered until they put in dedicated effort to explore different areas and subjects. It is through diligent work and experimentation that individuals stumble upon these hidden talents and cultivate them into something extraordinary. In this sense, hard work becomes the catalyst for unlocking one's full potential.

Hard work instills discipline and self-motivation. By consistently setting goals and working towards them, individuals develop a habit of discipline that spills over into all areas of their lives. This discipline allows them to stay focused, determined, and resilient in the face of challenges. Self-motivation, fueled by the rewards and satisfaction that come from hard work, becomes a powerful force that propels individuals forward, even in the absence of external pressures or recognition.

Importantly, hard work also fosters a growth mindset. When individuals actively engage in hard work, facing setbacks and overcoming obstacles along the way, they develop a belief in their ability to improve and grow.

Possessing a growth mindset allows people to welcome difficulties, see setbacks as opportunities to learn, and continue striving even when confronting hardships. It shifts the focus from fixed abilities to the belief that effort and dedication can lead to continuous growth and improvement.

Hard work cultivates a sense of ownership and pride in one's achievements. When individuals invest significant effort and time into their pursuits, they develop a deep sense of ownership over their success. They value the results achieved through their hard work, knowing that it was their determination and perseverance that brought them to where they are. This sense of ownership instills a greater appreciation for the journey and builds resilience to withstand any forthcoming challenges.

Additionally, hard work fosters qualities such as humility, empathy, and gratefulness. Through the process of working hard, individuals gain an understanding of the efforts required for success, allowing them to appreciate the achievements of others. They develop empathy towards those who face challenges and setbacks, knowing firsthand the struggle it takes to overcome them. Hard work often leads to a deep sense of gratitude for opportunities, mentors, and the support received along the way, reinforcing the importance of humility in the face of accomplishments.

In conclusion, the chapter "Hard work beats talent when talent doesn't work hard" emphasizes the significance of hard work in achieving success. It highlights the importance of consistent effort, resilience, discipline, and a growth mindset. Regardless of the level of talent one possesses, it is through hard work that individuals can truly tap into their latent potential, surpass expectations, and excel in their chosen field.

14

THE PAIN YOU FEEL TODAY WILL BE

THE STRENGTH YOU FEEL TOMORROW

In life, we all encounter pain and difficulties. It is an unavoidable truth of human experience. But what sets champions apart is their ability to not only endure but to embrace and overcome the pain they face. They recognize that pain is not the end, but rather a transformative force that has the potential to shape them into stronger, wiser, and more resilient individuals.

Physical pain, in all its manifestations, is an integral part of our existence. It can come in the form of injuries, illness, or the discomfort that accompanies pushing our bodies to their limits. When we embark on a journey of physical growth and challenge, whether it is through intense workouts, sports, or adventurous pursuits, we inevitably encounter pain. It is in these moments that champions are born.

By pushing ourselves physically, not only do we test the limits of our bodies, but we also test the limits of our minds. We face moments of excruciating discomfort when our muscles scream for us to stop, our lungs gasp for air, and every fiber of our being begs for respite. In those moments, champions find solace in discomfort, recognizing that pain is a teacher and a catalyst for growth.

Through consistent dedication and unwavering determination, champions push through the pain. They train their bodies to adapt, to become stronger, fitter, and more resilient. And as they conquer the pain they once feared, its power begins to diminish, and a new strength takes its place.

But physical pain is only one facet of human experience. Emotional pain, too, is a formidable force that shapes and defines us. It can arise from a myriad of sources – heartbreak, loss, trauma, and disappointment. It possesses the ability to shatter us to our cores, leaving behind fragments of our former selves.

Champions understand that emotional pain cannot be ignored or avoided. It demands acknowledgment and healing. They confront their demons head-on, diving deep into the depths of their psyche, untangling the intricacies of their emotions. It is an arduous journey, full of introspection and self-reflection, but it is through this process that true healing emerges.

To heal emotional pain, champions must face their vulnerabilities and confront the darkness within themselves. They must learn to embrace the pain, to sift through its layers, and extract the wisdom buried within. This process often requires support, whether it is from trusted friends, family, or mental health professionals. Champions understand that seeking guidance is not a sign of weakness but rather a testament to their strength and willingness to grow.

Within the crucible of emotional pain lies a remarkable opportunity for transformation. It teaches us empathy and compassion, allowing us to connect with others who are also struggling. Through our own suffering, we gain the ability to reach out and support those who are navigating their own painful journeys.

The path of pain is not linear or straightforward. It ebbs and flows, sometimes crashing against the shores of our lives with relentless force, while at other times receding into the whispers of memory. It is an ongoing process of self-discovery and self-actualization, as we learn to navigate the complexities of our own narratives.

But within this journey lies immense strength and resilience. The pain we feel today is not meant to break us but rather to shape us into the best versions of ourselves. It is a catalyst for growth and transformation, calling forth the depths of our character and fortitude.

So, embrace the pain, both physical and emotional. Embrace the challenges and hardships that come your way. Embrace the discomfort and the struggle, for within those moments lies the opportunity for immense growth and personal development.

Remember, the pain you feel today will be the strength you feel tomorrow. So, keep pushing, keep striving, and never give up. Your future self will thank you for persevering through the trials and tribulations, emerging stronger and more resilient on the other side.

15

THE DIFFERENCE BETWEEN ORDINARY AND

EXTRAORDINARY IS THAT LITTLE EXTRA

The difference between ordinary and extraordinary is not a mere distinction, but a vast chasm that separates those who dare to push their limits from those who settle for the status quo. It is a divide that penetrates the depths of our souls, where dreams wrestle with doubt and greatness coexists with the shadows of mediocrity. Within this nebulous and ever-shifting realm lies the genesis of transformation - the seeds of that little extra that can bridge the seemingly insurmountable abyss.

In the realm of sports, where triumph and defeat dance on the edge of a razor-thin line, the ordinary athlete is content to rely solely on their natural talent and abilities. They possess a gift, a predisposition for success, and yet they remain shackled by comfort and complacency. They believe that their inherent skills alone will carry them to victory, arrogantly dismissing the need for rigorous training, constant improvement, and relentless commitment. They overlook the fact that every step forward requires a hunger that propels them beyond the boundaries of average, beyond the limitations of perceived potential.

On the other hand, the extraordinary athlete stands as a beacon of inspiration amidst the sea of contenders. While they may have natural abilities, they recognize that raw talent alone does not lead to excellence. For them, giftedness is simply the foundation upon which outstanding achievement is built through dedicated effort. It is the tireless pursuit of improvement, the unyielding dedication to honing their craft that separates them from the masses.

They know that true champions are forged through the fires of sacrifice, the countless hours spent refining their skills when others rest. They embody the spirit of perseverance, undertaking additional sprints when their body pleads for rest, subjecting themselves to additional repetitions that transform ordinary into exceptional. Through a relentless drive to push beyond perceived limits, they rise above mere competence, forever etching their names in the annals of sports history.

Writing, too, resides in this realm of extraordinary endeavor. The ordinary writer seeks solace in the initial outpouring of thoughts onto paper, content with the raw expression of their thoughts and ideas. But the extraordinary writer knows that the true alchemy of words lies in the rewriting and refining process.

They understand the power of revision, the art of impeccability. They painstakingly polish every sentence, searching for inefficiencies and inconsistencies. No thought is left unexamined, no word is wasted. They mercilessly tear apart their own work, striving for clarity and resonance, and boldly ask themselves: "How can I make this better?" The extraordinary writer is not content with mere words; they yearn to evoke emotions, to paint vivid imagery, and to connect with readers on a profound level.

It is the relentless pursuit of perfection, that little extra attention to detail that elevates a work from ordinary to extraordinary. And in this quest for literary transcendence, they acknowledge that the mastery of their craft is not a destination, but a lifelong journey.

Beyond the realms of sports and writing, the ordinary and the extraordinary manifest in our daily lives, shaping the very fabric of our existence. In the domain of relationships, the ordinary person loves and cares, but often with limitations. They offer a shoulder to lean on and an ear to listen to but only to the extent that convenience allows. Their compassion is conditional, their empathy tentative.

Meanwhile, the extraordinary individual leaps beyond these emotional boundaries, extending their capacity for compassion even when it demands sacrifice. They embrace vulnerability, finding strength in their ability to connect with others on a deeper level. They seek to lift others higher, to offer a guiding hand during times of need. Through their little extras of kindness and generosity, they sow the seeds of profound connections that transcend the ordinary experiences of existence. It is their unwavering commitment to the well-being of others that reverberates throughout their interactions, forever changing the lives of those they touch.

In our professional lives, where the ordinary worker diligently completes their tasks and fulfills their responsibilities, the extraordinary individual reaches for the stars. They recognize that true innovation and growth lie in pushing boundaries, stepping out of comfort zones, and going above and beyond.

The ordinary settle into routines, finding solace in the familiarity of their spheres. But the extraordinary thrives on breaking free from the shackles of convention, embracing discomfort as a catalyst for change. They willingly take on additional responsibilities, eager to contribute their unique skills and talents in ways that surpass expectations. They are driven by a ceaseless thirst for knowledge, for constant improvement, and for the relentless pursuit of excellence.

It is this hunger, this little extra effort, which propels them toward success and distinguishes them from the mediocrity that saturates the professional landscape. They defy limitations, shattering glass ceilings and fostering environments of boundless possibility. And in doing so, they inspire others to transcend their own self-imposed restrictions.

In the end, the difference between ordinary and extraordinary is not a single, momentous feat, but the culmination of a thousand little extras. It is the fusion of passion and perseverance that ignites a spark within us, fueling the unwavering commitment to surpass our own limitations. It is the ability to silence the tantalizing whispers of mediocrity and embrace the call of greatness.

When we consistently practice these small, seemingly insignificant acts, when we choose to embrace discomfort and take steps beyond what is expected, the ordinary becomes extraordinary, and the extraordinary becomes the legacy we leave behind. Life, after all, is a symphony composed of countless individual notes - it is up to us to infuse each one with that little extra that transforms it from an ordinary sound into a masterpiece.

16

DOUBT KILLS MORE DREAMS THAN FAILURE EVER WILL

Doubt, the silent assassin of dreams, lurks in the shadows, waiting to pounce on our deepest desires and aspirations. It feeds on our insecurities and fears, sowing seeds of uncertainty that can stifle our progress and hinder our success. Many individuals, in their pursuit of greatness, succumb to the paralyzing grip of doubt, allowing it to dominate their thoughts and derail their dreams.

But what is doubt? It is a nagging voice that whispers incessantly, planting seeds of disbelief in our minds. It questions our abilities, our worthiness, and our chances of achieving our goals. It manifests itself in the form of self-criticism, comparing ourselves to others, and dwelling on past failures. Doubt can transform the most vibrant dreamer into a cautious skeptic, turning their aspirations into mere fantasies.

The human mind is a complex labyrinth, susceptible to the mazes created by doubt. It takes root in our thoughts, clouding our judgment and obscuring our vision. Doubt erodes our confidence, leaving us feeling inadequate, unworthy, and ill-prepared to face the challenges that await us. It feeds on our vulnerabilities, exploiting our deepest fears and insecurities.

Yet, doubt is not an inherent condition. It is a byproduct of our experiences, an accumulation of the times we have been let down or fallen short. It is born out of fear—fear of failure, fear of judgment, fear of disappointment. Doubt arises when we allow the expectations and opinions of others to define our worth and our potential. It takes hold when we become disconnected from our true selves, losing sight of our unique abilities and strengths.

To conquer doubt requires a journey of self-discovery and introspection. We must cultivate a deep-rooted sense of self-awareness, becoming intimately familiar with our passions, capabilities, and values. Through this deep understanding, we can build a solid foundation of self-belief that becomes impervious to doubt's attempts to undermine us.

Surrounding ourselves with a tribe of believers becomes paramount on this quest. Those who support and inspire us, who see our potential even when we cannot, are the anchors that keep us grounded in our dreams. Their unwavering belief acts as a shield against doubt, reminding us of our worthiness and our capacity for greatness. In their presence, doubt withers away, unable to withstand the collective strength of our supporters.

However, despite the support and self-awareness we may acquire, doubt does not easily relinquish its grip. It is a persistent adversary that rears its head time and time again. We must be prepared to face it head-on, armed with resilience and determination. This battle against doubt requires us to develop a growth mindset—a perspective that sees failure not as an end, but as a path toward growth and eventual success.

When doubt takes hold, we must examine the evidence that fuels its fire. More often than not, we will discover that these doubts are built on a foundation of skewed perceptions and misinterpreted experiences. Through objective evaluation of our doubts, we can dismantle their power, replacing them with a newfound sense of clarity and confidence.

Taking proactive steps to confront our doubts is essential. We must actively challenge the negative self-talk that fuels doubt, replacing it with positive affirmations that reinforce our abilities and worth. Surrounding ourselves with positive role models and seeking out learning opportunities can also help to alleviate doubt by expanding our knowledge and skill set.

Embracing discomfort becomes a powerful weapon against doubt. Stepping outside our comfort zones, we become intimately acquainted with the unknown. By fearlessly confronting the challenges and uncertainties that lie before us, doubt loses its grip. It is through these experiences of growth and learning that we build unshakable confidence and resilience.

In the grand tapestry of life, doubt is but a thread, one that can only hinder our progress if we allow it to. It is our choice whether to succumb to its insidious whispers or to rise above them. Doubt may be a natural byproduct of our aspirations, but it does not define us. We are not products of doubt, but rather courageous souls with limitless potential.

So, my fellow dreamers, let us embark on this journey with unwavering determination, refusing to let doubt be the victor. Let our dreams soar higher, carried by the winds of unwavering belief in ourselves. Each step we take, no matter how small or uncertain, is a testament to our resilience and courage. We shall defy doubt's attempts to extinguish our dreams and carve a path toward greatness. Together, we shall conquer doubt and embrace the fulfillment that awaits us on the other side.

17

EVERY PRACTICE IS A CHANCE TO GET BETTER

In the world of champions, there is a fundamental belief that every practice is an opportunity for growth and improvement. It is not just about going through the motions or ticking the boxes; it is about fully committing oneself to the process of becoming better than one was yesterday.

When the bright lights shine and the crowd roars, champions know that it is their countless hours of practice that have prepared them for this defining moment. They understand that practice is not just a repetition of the same actions; it is a deliberate and purposeful act of refining their skills, honing their technique, and building the resilience needed to excel.

Each practice session is a chance to push limits and test boundaries. The relentless pursuit of improvement demands embracing challenges and pushing past comfort zones. It requires dedication, discipline, and an unwavering commitment to excellence.

Physical practice is crucial, but champions know that mental practice is just as vital. They recognize that the mind plays a significant role in achieving success. They cultivate their mental strength, developing focus, concentration, and the ability to block out distractions. This mental fortitude not only helps them perform under pressure but also enables them to approach practice with a heightened level of intention and purpose.

Amidst the physical exertion and mental focus, one must not forget the importance of emotional practice. Emotions can greatly impact performance, positively or negatively. Champions learn to channel emotions effectively, transforming nervousness into excitement and frustration into determination. They master the art of self-awareness, recognizing their emotional state and using it as fuel to drive towards their goals.

Embracing a growth mindset during practice is crucial. Rather than seeing errors as failures, they can be viewed as opportunities for growth and pathways toward progress. Mistakes allow us to learn and get better, acting as springboards that propel us forward on our journey of improvement. Each error becomes an opportunity to learn, adjust, and enhance performance. Champions use mistakes as valuable feedback to identify areas for growth and make necessary adjustments to their approach. They understand that progress is not always linear and that setbacks are merely temporary obstacles on the path to success.

To make practice purposeful and effective, setting specific goals is essential. These goals act as guiding stars, illuminating the path to improvement. Whether it is mastering a new technique, improving speed and agility, or enhancing accuracy, each practice session should bring one closer to achieving these goals. However, champions know that the process is just as significant as the outcome. They find joy and fulfillment in the pursuit of their goals, rather than solely focusing on the end result.

Practice is not just about the physical and technical aspects; it also involves strategic thinking. Champions study their craft meticulously, analyzing opponents, and strategizing their approach. They dissect every aspect of their performance, seeking areas to capitalize on and opportunities to gain an edge. Practice, for them, is an opportunity to fine-tune their game plan, sharpen their decision-making skills, and adapt to different scenarios.

Reflection is a powerful tool in the practice process. After each practice session, take the time to evaluate performance objectively. Identify strengths that can be further capitalized on and areas that require improvement. Seek feedback from coaches, mentors, or teammates, and use their insights to refine skills and technique. Champions understand that the continuous cycle of reflection and refinement is key to progress.

True excellence is not an innate gift; it is the result of dedication, perseverance, and an unwavering commitment to practice. Talent alone cannot guarantee greatness; it is the relentless pursuit of improvement that sets champions apart. They understand that success is not a destination, but a continual evolution fueled by practice.

So, the next time one steps onto the field, court, or stage, remember that every practice is a chance to get better. Embrace the opportunity, unleash your full potential, and let each practice session be a step forward on your journey towards excellence. It is in these moments of commitment and dedication that true champions are born, and greatness is achieved.

18

MAKE YOUR SWEAT YOUR BEST ACCESSORY

In the journey toward success, one often encounters obstacles, challenges, and moments of doubt. It is during these times that true champions emerge and rise above the rest. To achieve greatness, one must be willing to put in the effort, the hours, and the dedication that it takes to reach their goals.

Sweat is a symbol of hard work, perseverance, and commitment. It is tangible evidence of the effort exerted in the pursuit of success. Each drop of sweat represents a step closer to victory, a step closer to achieving greatness.

When you make your sweat your best accessory, you embrace the physical and mental challenges that come with pursuing your dreams. You understand that the road to success is not an easy one and that there will be times when it feels overwhelming or impossible to continue. But it is in those moments that you push through, knowing that every drop of perspiration is bringing you closer to your goals.

Sweat is more than just a bodily function; it is a symbol of determination and resilience. It shows that you are willing to push yourself beyond your limits, step out of your comfort zone, and give your all in the pursuit of excellence.

The beads of sweat that trickle down your face and stain your clothes serve as a constant reminder that you are actively engaged in the process of growth and transformation. They represent the sacrifices made, the struggles faced, and the victories achieved. Each drop signifies the moments of self-doubt conquered, fear overcome, and resilience honed in the face of adversity.

There is a certain beauty in sweat, a rawness that comes from pushing your body and mind to their limits. It is a testament to your commitment and a reminder of the sacrifices made along the way. This physical manifestation of your effort becomes a visual representation of your inner strength and unwavering determination.

But sweat is not just a symbol of hard work; it is also a teacher. It teaches you the importance of discipline, of pushing through the discomfort and embracing the grind. Each droplet that falls from your brow carries with it a lesson, a reminder to keep going even when the odds seem insurmountable.

Moreover, sweat acts as a catharsis, a release of pent-up emotions and stress. As you sweat, you free yourself from the burdens that weigh you down, allowing your mind to clear and refocus on your goals. It is in these moments of physical exertion that you find mental clarity, enabling you to problem-solve, strategize, and find creative solutions to the challenges you face.

Sweat is a unifier; it is the great equalizer. It does not discriminate based on status, background, or talent. It is an undeniable result of the effort put forth, a testament to the fact that success is not reserved for a select few but available to anyone willing to work for it. In the realm of sweat, everyone is equal, everyone must put in the work, and everyone has the opportunity to succeed.

When you embrace your sweat as your best accessory, you harness its power and unlock your full potential. You understand that success is not just about talent or luck but about the relentless pursuit of improvement. You become immune to excuses, unyielding in your dedication, and you transform setbacks into stepping-stones towards greatness.

The moments of sweat-soaked determination are not easy, but they are worth it. They are the defining moments that shape you into the person you aspire to be. When you choose to embrace your sweat, you are making a conscious decision to commit, to push yourself, and to strive for more.

So, as you embark on your journey towards success, remember to make your sweat your best accessory. Embrace the challenges, push your limits, and never shy away from hard work. When you see drops of sweat on your brow, know that they are not signs of weakness but rather signs of strength and determination. Let your sweat be a reminder that you are on the path to greatness and that every drop brings you one step closer to achieving your dreams.

19

FALL DOWN SEVEN, GET UP EIGHT

Life is a tumultuous journey, woven with moments of triumph and moments of defeat. Like a never-ending rollercoaster ride, it propels us upward only to send us crashing back down, testing our resolve, and challenging our spirit. When faced with adversity and failure, it is easy to succumb to the weight of disappointment, to lose faith in our abilities, and question the path we have chosen. Yet, true champions are not forged through the absence of challenges, but through the unwavering strength and resilience they display when faced with setbacks. It is in the moments of defeat that we truly have an opportunity to learn, to grow, and to rise stronger than ever before.

The Japanese proverb, "Fall down seven times, get up eight," encapsulates the essence of perseverance and determination. It reminds us that failure is not a measure of our worth, but rather an invitation to gather our strength and forge a renewed path forward. This powerful saying teaches us that resilience is not a single act, but a continuous journey of self-discovery and growth.

When we fall, whether it is due to a personal failure, a professional setback, or an unexpected life event, we gain a special perspective—one that can only be attained through experiencing the depths of disappointment. It is during these moments that we are forced to confront our vulnerabilities, acknowledge our limitations, and recognize the areas in which we need to improve. Through the darkness of failure, a flickering light emerges, providing us with invaluable insight and motivation to rise once again.

Each fall shapes us in profound ways, amplifying our determination and fanning the flames of our ambition. It teaches us that success is not a linear path but a winding road laden with obstacles. It reminds us that every achievement of greatness is preceded by countless moments of doubt, rejection, and hardship. It is through these falls that we develop resilience, grit, and a tenacious spirit that refuses to accept defeat.

In the depths of failure, we are humbled. We are forced to confront the uncomfortable truth that we are not invincible, that our dreams and aspirations may not manifest as easily as we had hoped. It is in these moments that our character is tested, our resolve is fortified, and our true strength is revealed. For it is in our ability to rise from the ashes that we reveal our true potential—an indomitable spirit capable of conquering any obstacle.

The act of getting up is not merely a physical endeavor but a profound transformation of self. It requires harnessing the inner strength, resilience, and faith to continue moving forward even in the face of uncertainty. It demands unwavering belief in one's abilities and a refusal to be defined by temporary setbacks. To get up is to accept the imperfections, the bumps and bruises, and to embrace them as tutors on the path to excellence.

In this intricate dance between falling and rising, we become intimately acquainted with our own vulnerabilities and strengths. The falls, though painful, serve as catalysts for growth, instilling within us a sense of unwavering determination and an unyielding spirit. They remind us that success is not bestowed upon the faint of heart but rather reserved for those willing to put forth the unrelenting effort necessary to overcome obstacles.

Each fall becomes an opportunity for personal reflection, introspection, and improvement. It is within our ability to embrace failure as a process that will unlock our true potential and set us on a course towards greatness. We learn to adjust, to adapt, and to rise stronger and more resilient than we were before.

So, when life knocks you down, remember the wisdom of this profound proverb. Fall seven times, get up eight. Embrace the falls as moments of growth, use them as fuel to ignite the fire within you, and rise stronger than ever before. Let the rhythm of your determination guide you, and let it resound with unwavering strength and unwavering belief. For it is in rising from the depths that we discover our true power, ready to conquer the challenges that lie ahead.

20

THE ROAD TO SUCCESS IS ALWAYS UNDER CONSTRUCTION

Success is not a fixed destination; it is a continuous journey that weaves its way through the tapestry of our lives, leaving an indelible mark on our souls. Like a symphony composed of ups and downs, trials and triumphs, the road to success is a masterpiece in progress, requiring unwavering commitment, resilience, and an insatiable thirst for personal growth.

In the realm of construction, roads are not built overnight. They undergo meticulous planning, precise calculations, and strategic implementation. Architects and engineers unite their creative minds and technical expertise to design a path that can withstand the test of time. Similarly, on our individual journey towards success, we too must take the time to introspect, define our goals, and chart our course with careful consideration.

As we set out on this winding road, we must equip ourselves with the tools and resources necessary for the journey ahead. Just as construction workers carry their toolbox, filled with hammers, wrenches, and saws, we must arm ourselves with knowledge, skills, and a passion for continuous learning. Learning becomes the cornerstone of growth, empowering us to adapt to changing circumstances, overcome obstacles, and strive for excellence.

But the road to success is not a solitary one. Collaboration and support from others are the beams that hold our dreams aloft. Just as construction workers collaborate, lending their expertise and strength to one another, we too must surround ourselves with a network of individuals who believe in our vision and lift us higher. A community of mentors, peers, and loved ones provides guidance, encouragement, and accountability, ensuring we remain focused and driven.

No construction project is void of challenges. Construction sites are often met with unexpected hurdles such as inclement weather, budget constraints, and material shortages. But it is precisely these challenges that test our resolve and forge our character. Adversity becomes the scaffolding upon which we build our resilience, teaching us valuable lessons in perseverance, problem-solving, and adaptability. It is within the crucible of challenge that we discover our true strength and tenacity.

Just as construction workers assess their progress and adjust, we too must frequently evaluate our own growth and make necessary course corrections. Introspection becomes the compass that guides us forward, alerting us to areas for improvement and propelling us toward personal development. Self-reflection allows us to uncover our passions, values, and unique strengths, aligning them with our overarching goals to create synergy in our pursuits.

The road to success is not a linear progression, but rather a meandering path that leads us through multiple phases of our lives. Like a construction project that undergoes different stages, from excavation to foundation laying, framing to finishing touches, our journey crosses various seasons of exploration, consolidation, honing, and expansion.

Along this ever-evolving road, we encounter moments of self-doubt and uncertainty. The foundations we once trusted might begin to crumble, leaving us vulnerable to the winds of doubt that threaten to blow us off course. Yet, it is precisely in these moments that we must tap into reserves of self-belief and resilience, for it is during these times that we can rebuild and reinvent ourselves from the ground up.

As we navigate the twists and turns of our personal construction project, we must hold onto our dreams with relentless determination.

Just as perseverance is required when faced with unforeseen delays or setbacks during construction, we too must persist despite the obstacles that lie before us. The road to success is rarely smooth, but it is the challenges we overcome that propel us forward, transforming us into the best version of ourselves.

The metaphor of construction reminds us that success is not a destination but rather an ongoing process of growth, development, and self-discovery. It teaches us that our journey is unique, shaped not only by our achievements but also by the wisdom gained from our failures and setbacks.

As we continue our individual construction projects towards success, let us embrace the beauty within the process itself. Let us find solace in knowing that we are not tasked with reaching a fixed endpoint, but rather with continuously evolving, improving, and leaving a lasting legacy. The road to success is a transformative voyage, one that molds us into the architects of our own destinies, and as we work diligently and passionately, we pave the way for a future that exceeds our wildest dreams.

21

FOCUS ON THE JOURNEY, NOT THE DESTINATION

In a world that emphasizes the importance of end results, it is easy to get caught up in the desire for success. We set goals, we strive for achievements, and often, we measure our worth based on reaching those milestones. However, in the pursuit of our goals, we often overlook the beauty and growth that comes from the journey itself.

The journey, with all its twists and turns, challenges, and triumphs, is where the magic truly happens. It is a transformative process that shapes not only our external circumstances but also our internal landscape. It pushes us to step out of our comfort zones, confront our fears, and unlock our hidden potential.

At the start of any journey, we often find ourselves filled with excitement, hope, and a sense of determination. It is during this initial phase that we lay the groundwork for what lies ahead. We set our intentions, make plans, and visualize our desired outcome. This forward-looking mindset ignites a spark within us, propelling us forward and giving us the momentum to take that first step.

As we venture further into the journey, we encounter challenges that test our resolve. These obstacles are not mere roadblocks but growth opportunities. They force us to reassess our strategies, develop new skills, and tap into our well of resilience. While these challenges may feel difficult at the moment, they offer valuable lessons that shape our character. We learn the power of perseverance, adaptability, and inner strength, which becomes a wellspring of courage that we draw upon for future hurdles.

But it is not only through overcoming challenges that we grow. The journey also presents us with unexpected surprises, serendipitous moments, and chance encounters that broaden our horizons and deepen our understanding of the world. It is in these moments of spontaneity that we learn to embrace the unknown, to open ourselves up to new experiences, and to see the world through a different lens.

As the journey progresses, the outer landscape may change, but the inner transformation becomes more profound. We shed layers of self-doubt and limiting beliefs, allowing our true potential to emerge. We become acquainted with our passions, talents, and purpose, often uncovering hidden abilities that we never knew existed. The journey becomes a vehicle not only for achieving external goals but also for self-discovery and personal growth.

The path we travel on is not always clear. We may face forks in the road, unsure of which direction to take. These moments of decision can be pivotal as they require deep reflection and introspection. We must listen to our intuition, align with our core values, and trust that the choices we make will lead us closer to our desired destination. It is in these moments of uncertainty that we learn to trust ourselves and lean into the guidance of our inner compass.

In this complex tapestry of the journey, we also find ourselves surrounded by fellow travelers. Some join us for a short time, while others become lifelong companions on this shared adventure. These connections, forged through mutual support, empathy, and understanding, create a sense of belonging and community that nourishes our souls. We learn from each other's experiences, celebrate one another's victories, and provide a helping hand when the road becomes arduous. Together, we learn and grow, support and uplift, and find solace in knowing that we are not alone.

As the journey unfolds, we begin to realize that the destination we once fixated on is no longer the sole measure of success. The destination is merely a point in space and time, a culmination of our efforts and aspirations. But true fulfillment lies not in reaching that destination but in the growth, the learning, and the transformation that occurs along the way.

The journey becomes a metaphor for life itself. It teaches us resilience, patience, and gratitude for every step taken. It reminds us to savor the small joys, to appreciate the beauty of the present moment, and to embrace the inevitable changes that occur along the way. It is through the journey that we weave the threads of our own unique story, crafting a narrative rich in experience, lessons, and personal evolution.

As you embark on your own journey, remember to embrace it fully. Embrace the challenges, the setbacks, and the unexpected detours. Embrace the moments of doubt, for they are opportunities to reaffirm your commitment. And most importantly, embrace the beauty of the journey itself, for it is through this process that you discover who you truly are, uncover your purpose, and find fulfillment in a life well-lived.

22

YOU ARE STRONGER THAN YOU THINK

In the depths of our souls, where the raw emotions and desires reside, we often discover an untapped well of strength that is waiting to be harnessed. It is a strength that goes beyond the physical and encompasses the vast expanse of our inner world. This reservoir of fortitude is fueled by our unwavering determination, unwavering belief, and unwavering courage.

Throughout the journey of life, we encounter countless hurdles and setbacks, each one a unique test of our character. They may come in the form of personal disappointments, heart-wrenching losses, or the crushing weight of societal expectations. These challenges might appear insurmountable, casting shadows of doubt over our capabilities. But it is in these very moments, amidst the chaos and uncertainty, that our strength truly comes to light.

Physical strength, although formidable, is merely the tip of the iceberg. It is the mental strength that accompanies it, the power of the mind to endure and persevere that propels us forward. It is the unwavering belief that we are capable, despite the odds, and the understanding that failure is not an endpoint, but merely a detour on the path to success.

In the face of adversity, we must tap into the reservoir of mental strength within us. It is this strength that allows us to take setbacks as opportunities for growth and to view challenges as pathways to greatness. With a steadfast determination, we push through fatigue, overcome self-doubt, and emerge stronger on the other side. It is the mental strength that enables us to forge new paths, to envision a brighter future, and blaze a trail for others to follow.

Emotional strength, perhaps the most vulnerable yet mighty of all, lies hidden within the depths of our hearts. It is the resilience to weather the storms of life, to feel the depths of pain and sorrow, and yet continue to embrace hope and love. It is through emotional strength that we find the courage to rebuild shattered dreams, heal wounds, and extend compassion to both us and others.

In the realm of emotional strength, vulnerability is not a weakness but a source of power. It is the willingness to be open and honest with our own emotions, to confront our fears, and to allow ourselves to feel the full spectrum of human experience. It is through this vulnerability that we learn empathy and understanding, connecting with others on a deeper level and creating bonds that withstand the test of time. Emotional strength teaches us to navigate the complexities of relationships, to forgive and be forgiven, and to find comfort in moments of solitude.

Spiritual strength binds together the fragments of our being, connecting us to something greater than ourselves. It is the unyielding faith that resides within us, the belief in a higher power or universal force that guides and supports us through the darkest of times. With spiritual strength by our side, we find solace in the understanding that the challenges we face are not thrust upon us without reason, but rather an opportunity for growth and enlightenment.

In our pursuit of spiritual strength, we embark on a journey of self-discovery and introspection. We seek wisdom in ancient texts, guidance from enlightened beings, and solace in sacred places. It is a journey that transcends the limitations of the physical world, allowing us to connect with our higher selves and tap into the infinite wisdom that resides within.

And so, when faced with adversity, we must turn inward and draw upon these deep wells of strength that we possess. We must challenge the negativities that hold us back and fuel our determination in the face of insurmountable odds. Believe in the power that resides within you, for it is far greater than you can imagine. Trust that every difficulty you encounter is shaping you into a stronger, wiser version of yourself.

Surround yourself with individuals who uplift and inspire you. Seek out those who have walked a similar path and can offer guidance and support. Remember that strength is not found solely within ourselves but can spring forth from the support and encouragement of others as well.

Reflect on the past, on the trials you have overcome, and on the hurdles you have already conquered. These experiences serve as a testament to the indomitable spirit that resides within you. Allow those triumphs to fuel your belief in your strength and resilience.

Amid life's chaotic tapestry, never forget that you are stronger than you think. Tap into the depths of your being, connect with your inner power, and let it guide you through the valleys and mountaintops of your journey. Embrace the challenges, for they are an invitation to step into your greatness and unleash the full extent of your strength.

In the end, it is not just about surviving or merely existing. It is about thriving and embracing the fullness of life with every ounce of strength we possess. Trust in yourself, believe in your capabilities, and never doubt the power that lies within you. For you are a force to be reckoned with, a breathtaking example of the extraordinary strength that resides within each one of us.

23

KEEP GRINDING, GREATNESS TAKES TIME

In a world that thrives on instant gratification and quick success, it is important to remember that greatness does not happen overnight. It is not a sprint; it is a marathon. Achieving greatness requires consistent effort, unwavering dedication, and a willingness to keep grinding even when the going gets tough.

The path to greatness is often filled with obstacles, setbacks, and moments of self-doubt. It is easy to become discouraged when things do not go as planned or when progress seems slow. But it is during these moments that we must remind ourselves that greatness takes time.

Every great achievement in history has been the result of years of hard work, relentless perseverance, and a refusal to give up. Behind every successful individual lies a story of countless hours spent honing their craft, overcoming obstacles, and pushing beyond their limits. They understand that greatness is not handed to them; it is earned through endless effort and a commitment to improvement.

Keeping our eyes on the end goal can be challenging when progress seems slow or when we encounter setbacks along the way. However, it is important to remember that greatness is not defined by the speed at which we reach our goals but by the determination and resilience we display in the face of adversity.

Greatness takes time because it involves a process of growth, learning, and continuous self-improvement. It is about consistently showing up and putting in the work, even when it feels like we are not making progress. The key is to maintain unwavering commitment to the journey, regardless of the duration.

When we embrace the mindset of "keep grinding," we acknowledge that setbacks and obstacles are inevitable. We understand that progress may be slow, but we remain steadfast in our pursuit of greatness. We refuse to be discouraged by temporary setbacks or minor failures, knowing that they are merely milestones on the path to success.

The journey towards greatness is a transformative one. It molds us, challenges us, and shapes our character. It requires us to confront our fears, push beyond our comfort zones, and develop resilience in the face of adversity. The journey demands self-reflection, introspection, and a willingness to continuously learn and grow.

As we continue to grind towards greatness, it is crucial to celebrate small victories along the way. Recognize the progress we have made, no matter how small, and use that as fuel to keep moving forward. Each step, each effort, each learning experience contributes to our overall growth and brings us closer to realizing our full potential.

Moreover, the path to greatness is not a solitary one. Surrounding ourselves with like-minded individuals who believe in our dreams and support our journey is essential. They provide the encouragement, accountability, and inspiration we need to keep grinding. Collaboration, mentorship, and networking can open doors, expose us to new opportunities, and accelerate our path to greatness.

Furthermore, the quest for greatness requires us to cultivate certain habits and traits. We must cultivate discipline, consistency, and a strong work ethic. Greatness is not achieved through sporadic bursts of effort; it is the result of daily, deliberate actions aimed at improving ourselves and our craft. It is about setting goals, creating plans, and executing them with unwavering determination.

In addition, perseverance is a vital attribute on the path to greatness. This is the ability to keep going even when faced with adversity, rejection, or moments of self-doubt. Perseverance allows us to bounce back from setbacks, learn from failures, and stay focused on our long-term vision. It is not just about working hard; it is about staying committed to the process and believing in ourselves, even when the odds seem stacked against us.

Greatness also requires embracing patience and being mindful of the journey itself. It is about finding joy in the process, enjoying the small victories, and finding fulfillment in the daily grind. The road to greatness is not just about reaching the destination; it is about savoring each step along the way, appreciating the growth and transformation that occurs.

At times, the pursuit of greatness may feel arduous, lonely, or overwhelming. Doubts may creep in, questioning whether all the effort is worth it. During those moments, it is important to reconnect with our why - the deep-rooted passion and purpose that fuels our desire for greatness. This clarity will strengthen our resolve and serve as a constant reminder of our journey's significance.

Ultimately, greatness is not solely defined by external achievements but also by the impact we make on others and the world around us. Our journey towards greatness should be driven by a desire to make a positive difference, to leave a lasting legacy, and to inspire others to reach for greatness themselves.

So, if you are working towards greatness, keep going. Keep grinding, even when it feels like you are not getting anywhere. Trust the process and believe in your ability to reach the heights you aspire to. Remember that greatness takes time, and every step you take, no matter how small, is a step closer to achieving your goals.

Embrace the challenges, learn from the setbacks, and keep pushing forward. Stay focused, stay determined, and never lose sight of the greatness within you. Because, in the end, it is the ones who keep grinding that ultimately achieve true greatness.

24

WORK HARD IN SILENCE, LET SUCCESS MAKE THE NOISE

In a fast-paced world that values instant gratification and social media validation, it can be challenging to resist the urge to seek recognition and applause for our hard work. We are bombarded with messages that tell us we need to shout our accomplishments from the rooftops and prove our worth to others. However, beneath this culture of noise lies a profound truth: the most meaningful and transformative work is often done in silence.

When we choose to work hard in silence, we create a sacred space for our creativity and passion to flourish. Away from the distractions and pressures of the external world, we can delve deep into our craft and unlock the true potential within us.

For a writer, the act of creating is akin to a solitary pilgrimage. It is a journey that demands solitude, introspection, and a willingness to explore the vast depths of one's imagination. In the quiet of our minds stories take shape, characters are born, and emotions come alive. It is in these moments of pure creative immersion that we find our true voice, the unique expression of our souls.

But the beauty of working hard in silence extends beyond the act of creation itself. It seeps into every aspect of our artistic journey, shaping not only the final product but also the very essence of who we are as writers. In this silence, we confront our fears and insecurities, unraveling the layers of self-doubt that often plague creative minds. We learn to trust our instincts, to listen to the whispering of our inner voice, and to let it guide us toward our artistic truth.

There is a profound intimacy in the silence of creation. It is a dance between the conscious and the subconscious, where thoughts and emotions intertwine, giving birth to innovative ideas and fresh perspectives. It is in these moments of profound connection with ourselves that we discover the true depth of our creativity, unearthing hidden treasures buried within the recesses of our minds.

Through the process of working hard in silence, we cultivate a deep sense of discipline and unwavering commitment to our craft. It is not just about putting words on a page, but about honing our skills, perfecting our technique, and pushing the boundaries of our artistic capabilities. We learn to embrace the solitude that comes with the writer's life, finding solace in the company of our thoughts and the rhythmic tapping of keys or scratching of pen on paper.

But this journey is not without its challenges. As writers, we face the harsh realities of creative blocks, rejection, and self-doubt. It is during these moments that the silence becomes our refuge—a sanctuary where we can reflect, regroup, and find the strength to carry on. It is in silence that we rediscover our resilience, and our ability to rise from the ashes of doubt and continue our pursuit of excellence.

In the absence of external validation and recognition, we also develop a profound sense of humility. We understand that greatness is not measured solely by the number of accolades or followers we accumulate, but by the impact we have on others and the legacy we leave behind. This humility allows us to learn from others, to seek feedback and critique, and to continuously grow as writers and human beings.

Our journey of working hard in silence is not a solitary one. We are part of a vast community of creators, each on our own unique path, yet bound by the common thread of passion and dedication. While our individual journeys may be marked by moments of solitude, we find strength and inspiration in the stories and experiences of others. We become avid readers, sponges for knowledge, and seekers of inspiration—to further expand our horizons and to fuel our creative fire.

As we embrace the process of working hard in silence, we must also remember to celebrate our small victories along the way. The completion of a rough draft, the crafting of a compelling scene, and the positive feedback from a trusted beta reader—these moments remind us that progress is made one step at a time. Rather than seeking external validation, let us find joy in personal growth, the lessons learned, and the progress made. These moments of quiet triumph will serve as the foundation for the louder, more resounding successes that lie ahead.

Working hard in silence is not a sign of weakness or lack of ambition. It is an act of courage and self-belief. It requires an unwavering commitment to one's craft, a willingness to embrace solitude, and the resilience to persevere in the face of external pressures. So, continue to work diligently and passionately in silence, and trust that success will naturally emerge from the depths of our creative endeavors making an indelible impact on the world.

25

PAIN IS TEMPORARY,
BUT QUITTING IS FOREVER

Pain is a universal experience intricately woven into the fabric of existence. It permeates our lives touching every aspect of our being. From the physical sensations that signal our body's limits, to the emotional depths where heartache and sorrow reside, pain whispers its presence in every moment of our journey. And yet, despite its pervasive nature, pain holds the capacity to be an agent of transformation.

In its most palpable form, physical pain possesses the power to humble us. It reminds us of our mortal limitations, our bodies' fragility, and vulnerability. Whether it is the searing burn of a strained muscle, the piercing ache of a broken bone, or the persistent throbbing of an illness. Physical pain disrupts our routines and forces us to confront our mortality. It demands that we slow down, listen to the whispers of our bodies, and acknowledge the importance of self-care.

But physical pain is not solely a reminder of our limitations; it is also a testament to our resilience. It prompts the body to adapt, to heal, and to grow stronger. The discomfort we endure during exercise or athletic pursuits is the catalyst for growth, as muscles tear and mend, ultimately fortifying themselves.

In the face of injury or illness, our bodies activate their innate ability to regenerate and restore balance. As we emerge from the depths of physical pain, we embody a newfound appreciation for our bodies' potential and an understanding of the delicate symbiosis between pushing ourselves and nurturing our well-being.

On the emotional spectrum, pain immerses us in a world of intricate intricacies often hidden in the depths of our hearts. The heartache of lost love, the betrayal of trust, the longing for something unattainable – these emotional wounds are etched into our souls, defining the contours of our humanity. Emotional pain is a constant companion, shaping our perceptions, molding our identities, and molding our interactions with the world.

Emotional pain exposes the rawness of our vulnerabilities and exposes the intricate tapestry of our interconnectedness. It bridges the gap between individuals, revealing our shared experiences and illuminating the depth of our empathy. Those who have tasted the bitterness of heartbreak can empathize with the shattered dreams and the all-consuming grief of others. The experience of emotional pain offers an opportunity for profound growth as it awakens our compassion and teaches us to hold space for both our own suffering and the suffering of others.

Psychological pain, an often-silent companion, can be equally, if not more, debilitating. It permeates the realms of our thoughts, beliefs, and perceptions of self. Like a relentless adversary, it burrows into the crevices of our minds, sowing seeds of doubt, fear, and self-criticism. It is this form of pain that demands uncompromising self-reflection and introspection.

The maze of psychological pain can lead us down dark corridors of self-sabotage, perpetuating cycles of negativity, and limiting beliefs. It is here that we must summon our courage, explore the origins of our pain, and confront the narratives that hold us back. Through therapy, self-reflection, and inner work. We have the power to reframe our thoughts, rewrite our stories, and redefine our sense of self. In confronting psychological pain, we create space for healing, growth, and the emergence of a more empowered and authentic version of ourselves.

Beyond physical, emotional, and psychological realms, the human experience encompasses a profound spiritual dimension. The pain we experience in this sphere stems from a deep yearning for meaning, purpose, and connection. It is the unspoken anguish of feeling disconnected from something greater than ourselves of grappling with existential questions that defy easily graspable answers.

Spiritual pain is a call to reaffirm our faith, both in ourselves and in the intangible forces at play in the universe. It is a reminder that our journey is not one of isolated individuality but is intricately intertwined with the grand tapestry of existence. In embracing spiritual pain, we open ourselves to the possibility of transcendence, of finding solace in the unknown, and of rediscovering a sense of purpose. The pain of feeling disconnected can ultimately lead us to seek spiritual practices, explore philosophical teachings, or engage in acts of service that remind us of our interconnectedness with all beings.

Pain, in all its myriad forms, is a recurring thread woven throughout the tapestry of our lives. It challenges us, tests our resilience, and demands that we confront our vulnerabilities head-on. It is the chisel that shapes us, the forge that tempers our character, and the mirror that reflects our capacity for growth and transformation.

And so, as we traverse the valleys of pain, let us not be deterred by its temporary nature. Instead, let us embrace it as a catalyst for growth, a call to resilience, and a reminder of our boundless capacity to overcome. In the depths of pain, we uncover hidden reservoirs of strength, resilience, and determination that extend far beyond our perceived limitations. With every act of perseverance, we step closer to our true potential, embracing the profound beauty that emerges from the depths of our struggles.

In the face of pain, remember this: it is temporary, but the growth and wisdom that arise from persevering are everlasting. Embrace the journey, endure the pain, and emerge on the other side, stronger, wiser, and ready to embrace all that life has to offer.

26

TRAIN LIKE A BEAST, PERFORM LIKE A CHAMPION

In the world of sports, greatness is not achieved without hard work and dedication. Athletes who excel on the field, track, court, or any arena, know that success is earned through relentless training and unwavering commitment to their craft. To train like a beast is to go beyond the ordinary, pushing physical and mental boundaries to reach extraordinary levels of performance. It requires a deep understanding of one's potential and an unyielding drive to unlock it.

When you train like a beast, you become intimately familiar with the pain of pushing your body to its limits. You know that true progress lies just outside the comfort zone and tap into that knowledge every time you step onto the field. It is in those moments when your muscles scream for mercy, when fatigue threatens to consume you, that you realize the true power of the human spirit. It is the ability to push through the pain, to harness an indomitable will that sets you apart.

In your pursuit of excellence, each practice session becomes a deliberate opportunity for growth. You approach training with a methodical mindset, dissecting your strengths and weaknesses, and tailoring your workouts to address them. You seek out the guidance of coaches and mentors, embracing their wisdom and expertise to refine your technique and elevate your performance. You study film, analyzing your own movements, and those of your competitors to gain a competitive edge. You leave no stone unturned in your quest to become the best version of yourself.

Training like a beast requires unwavering discipline. You realize that success is not built on occasional bursts of effort, but rather on consistent, daily commitment to your goals. You understand the importance of structuring your training regimen, setting clear objectives, and staying accountable to yourself. You rise early in the morning, long before the sun paints the horizon, to squeeze in extra hours of practice. While others rest, you are honing your skills, expanding your endurance, building the physical and mental fortitude necessary for triumph.

But training like a beast is not a solitary pursuit. It is often cultivated in the crucible of team environments, where cohesion and camaraderie create a collective force that propels each athlete to new heights. You understand that being a champion is not solely about individual success but also about lifting up your teammates and fostering an environment of mutual support. You push each other to be better, to surpass limits previously thought unreachable, and together you forge a bond that stretches beyond the field.

As a beast in training, you recognize the significance of proper nutrition and recovery. Your body is a temple, a vessel for greatness, and you treat it as such. You understand the importance of feeding it with wholesome, nutrient-dense foods, fueling it for optimal performance. You prioritize rest, sleep, and recovery, allowing your muscles to heal and strengthen. In the pursuit of greatness, you are mindful of the delicate balance between pushing your limits and taking care of your body for the longevity of your career.

But true champions do not simply reside in the realm of training. They emerge when the stakes are highest, when the spotlight shines brightest. To perform like a champion is to rise above the pressure and expectation, to deliver when it matters most. It is the culmination of countless hours of training, mental preparation, and self-belief.

Performing like a champion requires unwavering focus and mental fortitude. It means blocking out the noise of the crowd, the distractions that threaten to derail your concentration. You tap into a deep reservoir of self-confidence, trusting in your abilities and the work you have put in. You stay poised, even in the face of adversity, adapting your game plan on the fly to seize the moment. Performing like a champion means channeling your energy into each play, each stroke, each step, fully immersing yourself in the present moment, and executing with precision.

To truly train like a beast and perform like a champion is to embody a growth mindset. It is about constantly seeking avenues for improvement and never settling for mediocrity. It is embracing failure as an opportunity to learn and grow, analyzing setbacks as steppingstones towards success. It is being open to feedback, receptive to constructive criticism, and continuously challenging yourself to be better. It is about cultivating resilience, bouncing back from defeats, and using them as motivation to push harder and reach new heights.

When you train like a beast and perform like a champion you become an inspiration to those around you. Your unwavering dedication and your relentless pursuit of excellence becomes a guiding light for others who witness your journey. You become a role model for aspiring athletes, a testament to the power of the human spirit and the possibilities that await when one commits wholeheartedly to their passion.

So, as you embark on your athletic journey, remember to train like a beast. Embrace the sweat, the grind, the sacrifice that comes with pushing your limits. Seek out knowledge, guidance, and the camaraderie of teammates who are on the same path. Fuel your body with the right nutrition rest and recovery. Develop mental fortitude and a growth mindset, knowing that greatness lies just beyond your comfort zone. And when it is time to perform, unleash the champion within you. Trust in the process, believe in yourself and leave it all on the field. In the end, success is not defined by victories alone, but by knowing that you gave it your all and left a legacy that will endure long after the final whistle has blown.

27

YOUR DEDICATION TODAY WILL BE YOUR LEGACY TOMORROW

In the journey to achieve greatness, it is essential to remember that every action, every effort, and every sacrifice you make today will leave behind a lasting impact on the world tomorrow. Your dedication is not simply about the present moment; it is about building a legacy that will resonate long after you are gone.

When you commit yourself to a goal or a dream, it is your unwavering dedication that will determine your success. It is the choice to show up every day, to put in the work, and to never settle for mediocrity that sets you apart from the rest. Your dedication is not just a fleeting motivation; it is a deep-rooted commitment to excellence.

Throughout history, we have witnessed the transformative power of dedication. The world's greatest innovators, leaders, and visionaries were not overnight successes; they were relentless in their pursuit of their dreams. Their dedication transcended mere talent or intelligence. It was a powerful force that propelled them forward, even when faced with adversity and discouragement.

They understood that dedication is not about achieving instant gratification; it is about having the patience and perseverance to withstand the challenges and setbacks that inevitably arise. It is about embracing inevitable failures as valuable lessons and using them as tools towards growth and improvement. Your dedication is not only the key to success, but also the catalyst for personal development and self-discovery.

The path to greatness is rarely straightforward. It is filled with winding roads, unexpected detours, and moments of doubt. It is during these times that your dedication shines the brightest. It is when you continue to push forward, despite the obstacles, that you demonstrate your unwavering commitment to your dreams. Your dedication becomes the fuel that propels you towards success, even in the face of immense challenges.

But dedication is not merely about personal achievement. It is about the responsibility that comes with excellence. It is through your dedication to your craft that you have the opportunity to touch hearts, challenge perspectives, and advocate for change.

Your dedication goes beyond the pursuit of personal success; it is about making a positive impact on the world around you. It is about using your platform and your voice to amplify important messages, shed light on social issues, and inspire others to take action. By staying dedicated to your purpose, you have the ability to spark movements, ignite passion, and leave an indelible mark on society.

Remember that dedication is not limited to a single endeavor or moment in time. It is a mindset, a way of life that permeates every aspect of who you are. It is about consistently giving your all, even when no one is watching. It is about showing up, putting in the work, and never settling for anything less than your best. Your dedication becomes the foundation upon which your legacy is built.

So, as you embark on your journey towards greatness, let your dedication be your guiding light. Embrace the challenges and setbacks as opportunities to grow and evolve. Cultivate a mindset that embraces lifelong learning and continuous improvement. Remember that the choices you make today will influence the impact you leave behind tomorrow.

Your dedication today will be your legacy tomorrow. It is not just about achieving personal success; it is about inspiring others, making a difference, and leaving a mark upon the world that will endure long after you are gone. Stay committed, stay focused, and never lose sight of the profound influence you have the power to create through your unwavering dedication.

28

NO EXCUSES, ONLY RESULTS

In the realm of champions, where dreams are transformed into realities and greatness is the currency of success, excuses are but a distant echo. They have no place within the minds of those who have embraced the journey of self-discovery and self-mastery. Champions understand that success is not a destination, but rather a continuous exploration of human potential, pushing the boundaries of what is believed to be possible.

Excuses, in their essence, represent a refuge from the discomfort of failure, a shield to protect our ego and preserve our sense of self-worth. They provide temporary solace, blinding us from the lessons that failure can teach. Yet champions have come to realize that true growth lies not in evading failure, but in embracing it wholeheartedly and extracting wisdom from its clutches.

When confronted with challenges, champions do not default to finding faults in external circumstances or placing the blame on others. Instead, they embark on an inward journey of self-reflection, seeking to understand their own role in the situation. They acknowledge that their actions, choices, and mindset shape the outcomes they experience. Taking full responsibility for their circumstances, champions proactively seek solutions, even when the odds seem insurmountable.

In the face of adversity, champions harness their resolve and tap into their inner strength to seek clarity and resilience. They do not allow external circumstances to define or limit their potential but boldly confront them with unwavering determination. By refusing to yield to the grip of excuses, they transcend their limitations and discover the true extent of their capabilities.

Champions understand that their journey is a canvas on which they author their own narrative. They refuse to be passive spectators in their own lives, instead stepping into the role of the protagonist who transforms challenges into opportunities for growth. Through this empowering mindset, they learn that setbacks are not defeats but mere learning experiences on the path to excellence.

Successful champions leverage their setbacks as catalysts for change. They learn from every stumble, every failure, and every moment of disappointment. Each experience becomes an invaluable lesson, propelling them forward with renewed determination. Because they understand that while excuses may momentarily shield them from judgment or discomfort, they ultimately restrict their growth and potential.

The pursuit of greatness demands an unwavering commitment to personal growth. Champions recognize the need for discipline, dedication, and persistent effort. Striving for excellence becomes a way of life, permeating every facet of their existence. They willingly embrace the sacrifices required to reach their goals, forsaking the fleeting pleasures of instant gratification in favor of the long-term satisfaction that comes with pursing their passions.

A champion's mindset is nurtured through self-discipline and a relentless focus on their goals. They cultivate habits that reinforce their commitment to progress, dedicating hours to deliberate practice, deepening their knowledge, and expanding their skill set. They understand that mastery is not a destination, but an ongoing journey and they consistently strive to push the boundaries of their capabilities.

In their quest for excellence, champions recognize the power of collaboration and surround themselves with like-minded individuals. They create a support system of mentors, coaches, and peers who challenge and inspire them to go beyond their perceived limits. They intuitively understand that shared success is amplified success and that the collective wisdom of a community can propel them towards their goals with astonishing speed.

In their pursuit of greatness, champions do not seek external validation or fame. True champions find fulfillment in the process itself, in the growth and transformation they experience along the way. They recognize that true success is not measured by material accolades but by the impact they have on others, their ability to inspire and uplift those around them. They understand that by shining their light, they ignite a spark in others and create a ripple effect that extends far beyond their own accomplishments.

No excuses, only results. This is the mantra of a champion. They have embraced the path less traveled, one that demands unwavering commitment, resilience in the face of adversity, and the relentless pursuit of personal growth. With every step forward, champions leave the realm of mediocrity behind and enter a world where dreams take flight and greatness becomes their eternal legacy.

29

VICTORY BELONGS TO THE MOST PERSEVERING

In the face of adversity, when the odds are stacked against you, it is the individuals who persevere that ultimately emerge victorious. This chapter delves deeper into the power of perseverance and explores its multifaceted aspects, providing a comprehensive understanding of how it can lead to triumph in the face of even the most challenging circumstances.

Life is not always a smooth journey; it is often paved with hurdles, obstacles, and setbacks that test our mettle. It is during these trying times that the power of perseverance shines brightest. It is a mindset that perseveres through adversity, a relentless determination that fuels progress, and an unwavering belief that triumph is possible, even in the face of seemingly insurmountable odds.

Perseverance begins with setting clear and meaningful goals. These goals serve as guiding stars, providing focus, motivation, and a sense of purpose as we navigate the uncertain terrain of life. Clear goals ensure that our efforts are directed towards what truly matters, empowering us to overcome obstacles and stay the course, even when it feels easier to give up.

But mere goals are not enough. Perseverance demands a strategic and systematic approach to overcoming challenges. It compels us to break down daunting tasks into smaller, more manageable segments, taking incremental steps forward even in the face of overwhelming odds. This approach not only enables progress but also allows for the development of essential skills, knowledge, and resilience along the way.

Resilience, often considered the bedrock of perseverance is the ability to bounce back from setbacks. It is the inner strength that enables individuals to stay strong, to keep going when others have already given up. Resilience is neither an inherent trait nor a fixed characteristic but rather an adaptability that can be developed through experience. Facing and overcoming adversity builds resilience, as we learn to cope, adjust, and grow stronger with each challenge we overcome.

An integral part of fostering perseverance is cultivating a growth mindset. This mindset is grounded in the belief that abilities and talents can be developed through dedication and hard work. It is a rejection of fixed notions of talent or intelligence and embraces the idea that failure is not a reflection of our worth but rather an opportunity for growth. By adopting this mindset, setbacks are not seen as roadblocks but as building blocks towards improvement and success. As we learn from our mistakes, we gain the insight and knowledge necessary to adapt and forge ahead with renewed determination.

Perseverance is not a solo endeavor. It often relies on the support and encouragement of others. Surrounding ourselves with a strong support system, whether it be mentors, friends, or loved ones, can provide the necessary motivation and guidance during challenging moments. These individuals can offer valuable insights, act as sounding boards, and lend a helping hand when things get tough. Sharing the journey with like-minded individuals fosters camaraderie, accountability, and a sense of collective strength, enhancing our ability to persevere through the most challenging circumstances.

Victory does not always come quickly or easily. It is often the culmination of years of dedication, hard work, and sacrifice. Perseverance requires staying on the course even when the journey becomes difficult or uncertain. It is during these moments of struggle that the most persevering individuals rise above the rest, fueled by their unwavering passion and resolve. They embrace each setback as an opportunity to learn and grow, continually adapting and refining their approach until victory is finally attained.

Perseverance is not limited to specific fields or industries. It transcends boundaries, as individuals from all walks of life embody this indomitable spirit. From the realms of science, art, sports, and literature, the stories of those who never gave up continue to inspire generations. These stories remind us that with perseverance, even the loftiest of dreams can be realized and the impossible can become possible. Whether it is the scientist dedicating years to their research, the artist relentlessly honing their craft, or the athlete enduring rigorous training regimes, the common thread among these individuals is their unwavering resolve to persevere, despite the challenges they face.

In conclusion, perseverance is not just an admirable quality; it is a mindset that can transform lives. It begins with setting clear goals, developing a strategic plan, and embracing a growth mindset. It requires resilience, a strong support system, and an unshakeable belief in oneself. Through perseverance, triumph becomes attainable, and dreams are transformed from mere wishes into reality. So, embrace the power of perseverance, and let it guide you through the challenges and setbacks of life. In the battle between perseverance and adversity, may your unwavering spirit emerge victorious, and may your journey become a testament to the triumph of the human spirit.

30

BELIEVE IN YOUR ABILITY TO SUCCEED, AND YOU WILL

Belief is a powerful force that can transform your life. It has the ability to shape your thoughts, emotions, and actions, influencing the trajectory of your journey towards success. When you truly believe in your ability to succeed, you unlock a world of possibility and potential propelling yourself towards greatness.

To cultivate unwavering belief in yourself, it is vital to foster a positive mindset that embraces self-empowerment and growth. Train your mind to focus on the strengths and abilities that make you unique. Remind yourself daily of the qualities that have contributed to your past accomplishments and recognize that they are indicators of the greatness that lies within you. By celebrating your achievements, no matter how big or small, you reinforce the belief that you are capable of overcoming any obstacle that comes your way.

While cultivating self-belief, it is essential to let go of self-doubt and negative self-talk. These destructive thoughts can hinder your progress and hold you back from reaching your full potential. Replace them with positive affirmations that reinforce your abilities and potential. Surround yourself with inspirational quotes, uplifting affirmations, and success stories to infuse your mind with positivity and motivation.

Moreover, self-belief is strengthened through personal growth and continuous learning. Embrace opportunities to expand your knowledge, acquire new skills, and enhance your abilities. Investing in yourself through courses, workshops, or mentorships can not only boost your confidence but also provide you with the practical tools required to succeed in your endeavors. Remember, growth is a lifelong journey, and each step you take towards personal development reinforces your belief in your ability to achieve greatness.

Setting clear and achievable goals is another integral aspect of developing self-belief. By defining what success looks like for you and breaking it down into smaller milestones, you create a roadmap that guides your actions. Celebrate every step forward, recognizing that each achievement reinforces your capability to succeed. Additionally, consider the challenges and obstacles you may encounter along the way. Preparing for potential setbacks and devising strategies to navigate them will fortify your belief in your ability to overcome any hurdle.

However, genuine self-belief does not eliminate the possibility of failure. It is important to see failure as part of the learning process and an opportunity for growth. Embrace failures as steppingstones, not stumbling blocks. Each setback provides valuable lessons, highlighting areas for improvement and refining your approach towards success. Learn from your mistakes, adjust your course, and persevere with the unwavering belief that you have what it takes to achieve your ambitions.

In conclusion, self-belief is a potent force that can propel you towards unimaginable success. Cultivate a positive mindset, acknowledge your strengths, and celebrate your past achievements. Seek personal growth opportunities, surround yourself with a supportive network, and set clear goals that align with your aspirations. Embrace challenges as opportunities for growth and never lose sight of the unwavering belief in your own potential. With determination, perseverance, and a steadfast belief in yourself, you have the power to shape your destiny and write the extraordinary story of your life.

31

CHAMPIONS ARE BUILT ON A FOUNDATION OF FAILURE

In the world of sports and indeed in life, failure is an omnipresent force. It looms over us, biding its time, ready to pounce on our greatest endeavors. It is the shadow that follows our every move, the unwelcome companion that often accompanies our journey towards success. Yet, it is through failure that we learn some of our most valuable lessons and grow into the champions we are destined to become.

Every great athlete, from the legendary tales of Michael Jordan soaring through the air to Serena Williams dominating the tennis court, has faced countless failures along their path to greatness. It is their ability to rise above these setbacks, to defy the odds, and to use their failures as motivation that sets them apart from the rest.

Failure is not a sign of weakness or incompetence; it is a sign of taking risks and pushing beyond our comfort zones. It is in those moments of defeat that we have the opportunity to reevaluate our strategies, to reassess our goals, and to strive for improvement. It is through failure that we are forced to confront our limitations and push ourselves to new heights.

But what separates champions from the rest is their mindset towards failure. Instead of succumbing to despair, champions rise from the ashes of their failures, fueled by a burning desire to prove themselves. It is an unwavering belief in their abilities and a refusal to let setbacks define them that propel them forward.

Champions understand that failure is not an endpoint but a turning point. It is a catalyst for growth and self-discovery. They utilize failure as a tool for introspection, diving deep into the depths of their souls to uncover the weaknesses that led to defeat. They analyze every misstep, every missed opportunity, and every flaw in technique, searching for the key to unlocking their true potential.

It is through failure that champions learn resilience, the ability to bounce back stronger and more determined than ever. They understand that true strength comes not from avoiding failure, but from embracing it as part of the journey. It is a constant battle against self-doubt, a reminder that the pursuit of greatness is never easy or linear.

Failure also teaches champions the value of perseverance. They develop the mental fortitude to keep pushing, to keep working towards their goals despite repeated setbacks. It is this unwavering commitment to their craft that sets them apart. They know that success requires blood, sweat, and tears, and that failure only fuels their desire to keep striving.

Perhaps most importantly, champions are not afraid to take risks. They understand that in order to achieve greatness, they must step outside of their comfort zones and push the boundaries of their abilities. Failure becomes an inevitable companion on their journey, but it is through these risks that the sweet taste of triumph is savored.

So, whether you are a budding athlete or a person striving for success in any aspect of life, remember that failure is not the end, but rather the beginning of a greater journey. Embrace your failures, learn from them, and let them shape you into the person you are destined to become.

In the words of basketball legend Michael Jordan, "I've missed more than 9000 shots in my career. I have lost almost three hundred games. Twenty-six times, I have been trusted to take the game-winning shot and missed. I have failed over and over and over again in my life. And that is why I succeed." Let these words resonate within you, echoing through the depths of your being, as a reminder that failure is a necessary and valuable part of your journey towards success.

32

SUCCESS IS THE SUM OF SMALL EFFORTS

REPEATED DAY IN AND DAY OUT

Success is a nuanced and intricate tapestry woven through a series of small efforts repeated day after day. It is the harmonious symphony of consistency and persistence, orchestrated to create an awe-inspiring masterpiece.

When we gaze at the achievements of renowned individuals, from towering figures of history to modern visionaries, it is easy to be captivated by their grandeur and overlook the countless small actions that led them there. We admire their accomplishments without fully appreciating the relentless commitment and unwavering dedication they invested to attain those heights.

Consider the artistry of famous painters. The masterpieces that hang in renowned galleries across the world are not the result of a few moments of genius; they are the culmination of countless brushstrokes painstakingly applied with precision and care. These artists spent years honing their craft, studying the techniques and styles of past masters, patiently perfecting their brushwork and experimenting with colors and textures. Each stroke was deliberate, purposeful, and a step toward mastering their art.

Similarly, great writers craft their novels, not through a miraculous surge of inspiration, but by dutifully sitting down day after day, word after word, shaping and refining their narratives. They know that creating compelling stories requires discipline and effort. They research, develop characters, plot intricate storylines, and revise endlessly, cutting and reshaping sentences and paragraphs until their words sparkle with brilliance.

success goes beyond the realm of artistry. In the domain of science, pioneering discoveries and paradigm-shifting breakthroughs are not birthed from eureka moments alone. They are the culmination of countless hours spent in laboratories, meticulously designing experiments, scrutinizing data, and analyzing results. Scientists pursue their investigations with unwavering curiosity, often spending months or even years toiling away before they stumble upon a significant finding. They understand that each small step contributes to the larger scientific endeavor and that success lies in the cumulative impact of dedicated and consistent effort.

Success is an intricate dance, choreographed by consistent and deliberate actions. It is the daily decision to wake up early, driven by an unwavering desire to push the limits of one's potential. It is the sweat and toil shed during hours of practice, the relentless pursuit of mastery that propels athletes to break records and achieve greatness. Behind the awe-inspiring acrobatics of a gymnast, the graceful leaps of a ballerina, or the precise swings of a golf champion lies a journey marked by countless hours of training, repetition, and overcoming physical and mental barriers.

But what happens when the path to success becomes riddled with obstacles and setbacks? It is in these moments that the true test of character emerges. Will we succumb to adversity, or will we rise above it? The small efforts repeated even in the face of resistance are the building blocks of resilience, fortifying our determination and shaping our ability to overcome challenges.

Successful individuals understand that success is not a sprint, but a marathon. It is a journey filled with peaks and valleys requiring unwavering determination and the ability to sustain long-term focus. It demands the wisdom to recognize that progress is not always linear, and that setbacks and failures are not roadblocks but steppingstones toward growth.

In the pursuit of success, the power of routine cannot be underestimated. Time and again, studies have shown that establishing daily rituals and habits increases productivity and enhances overall performance. By committing ourselves to consistent practice, we create an environment where success becomes inevitable. From the structured routines of the world's top CEOs to the habitual learning patterns of esteemed scholars, these individuals understand the importance of creating systems that promote continual growth and progress.

Let us not underestimate the significance of choice. Every day, we are faced with numerous decisions—some seemingly insignificant, others life-changing. The small efforts we repeat are a manifestation of the choices we make. Each moment presents an opportunity to choose actions that align with our aspirations and goals. The secret lies in the awareness of these choices and the deliberate selection of actions that bring us closer to our desired outcomes.

To embark on the path of success, it is crucial to define what success means to us personally. Success is a deeply personal journey, and its definition varies from one individual to another. While societal norms and external pressures may try to dictate our aspirations, true success comes from aligning our actions with our values, passions, and purpose. It is in finding fulfillment in our daily efforts that we truly experience the essence of success.

We must also recognize that success is not solely an individual endeavor but is intricately linked to the relationships we foster along the way. Collaborative efforts, support networks, and mentorship play a significant role in propelling individuals towards their goals. Successful people understand the importance of surrounding themselves with like-minded individuals who inspire and challenge them to reach new heights.

As we embark on our individual journeys towards success, let us remember that every action counts. In the grand tapestry of life, it is the consistent repetition of small efforts that shapes our destiny. Each step, no matter how small, has the potential to create a ripple effect that reverberates through time and space.

So, let us embrace the power of the mundane, the significance of the seemingly insignificant, and the beauty of the everyday. Let us recognize that success is not a destination but a continuous evolution. It is the gentle hum of progress, the melody composed by the daily symphony of our small efforts, that ultimately leads us to the pinnacle of achievement.

33

THE ONLY BAD WORKOUT IS THE ONE THAT DIDN'T HAPPEN

In the world of champions, where dreams are transformed into reality through sheer determination and relentless effort, there exists a universal truth: consistency is the key to success. It is an unwavering commitment to show up day after day, pushing yourself beyond your limits, and refusing to accept anything less than excellence.

Workouts, though they may seem like fleeting moments of physical exertion hold immense power. They are not merely exercises for the body; they are catalysts for personal growth and transformation. Within the rhythm of each repetition, and the pounding of each step, lies an opportunity to forge a stronger more resilient version of yourself.

At its core, a workout is a sacred act—an act of self-care and self-love. It is in these moments of physical exertion that we dig deep within ourselves tapping into reserves of strength and courage we never knew we possessed. It is a time when we confront our fears, insecurities, and doubts head-on, as we push past our perceived limitations and redefine the boundaries of our capabilities.

Motivation, that elusive force that often seems fleeting, is not the true driver behind progress. It is discipline that separates the champions from the average. It is the unwavering resolve to follow through with your commitment regardless of how you feel or the obstacles that may arise. While motivation comes and goes like a flickering flame, discipline keeps the fire burning brightly, guiding your every step toward your aspirations.

However, discipline alone is not enough. The mind and body function as a harmonious unit and it is crucial to cultivate a strong mental foundation to accompany physical exertion. A successful workout requires a mindset that embraces discomfort, celebrates challenge, and views adversity as an opportunity for growth. It demands focus, concentration, and a willingness to step outside the comfort zone.

The road to greatness is not always smooth; it is paved with challenges and setbacks. There will be days when the weights feel heavier, the treadmill feels endless, and the pool seems like an insurmountable distance. But it is precisely on those days, the days when inspiration feels distant, that the true champions rise to the occasion. They understand that greatness is not achieved solely on the days when everything aligns perfectly, but rather on the days when it seems impossible.

In those seemingly lackluster workouts where fatigue sets in and your body feels like it could collapse, you must remember one crucial truth: progress is not always linear. It is the accumulation of countless small victories, each of which may seem insignificant at the time. Every ounce of effort expended, no matter how minimal it may seem, adds up to creating a sturdy foundation upon which success is built.

Your workout is an investment—a steadfast commitment to your physical and mental well-being and to the realization of your goals. It is an investment that pays dividends far beyond the momentary sweat and exhaustion. It strengthens not only your muscles but also your character. It instills discipline, resilience, and grit into the very fabric of your being.

Every choice you make, and every action you take contributes to the story you are crafting. When you choose to prioritize your health and commit to your workouts, you are writing the narrative of a champion—one who embraces challenges, defies limitations, and continues to evolve into their most formidable self.

So, when the alarm clock rings too early, the weather turns unideal, or life's demands threaten to derail your progress, remember this: the only bad workout is the one that did not happen. Embrace the discomfort and fatigue as signs of growth. Embrace the journey, the journey towards becoming the best version of yourself. Trust that every workout, no matter how imperfect, brings you one step closer to the greatness that lies within you.

In those moments of doubt and weariness, summon your inner champion. Rise above excuses, ignore the nagging voice of resistance, and push forward. Keep showing up, and keep giving your all, for the road to success is not a destination but a lifelong journey. And with each step, with each workout, you are inching closer to the extraordinary life you were meant to live. Let your workouts be a testament to your dedication, a testament to the indomitable spirit that drives you. Workouts are not just exercises; they are manifestations of your commitment to a life well-lived.

34
WINNING ISN'T EVERYTHING, BUT WANTING TO WIN IS

Wanting to win is a complex and multifaceted aspect of human nature. It delves deep into the core of our desires and motivations, shaping our actions and defining our paths. While some may dismiss the desire to win as a shallow and superficial pursuit, it carries profound significance in our personal and collective journeys.

The yearning to win is deeply ingrained within us, stemming from our innate instinct to survive and thrive. Throughout history, humans have faced countless challenges, from securing food and shelter to competing for limited resources. In this context, the desire to win is a fundamental aspect of our survival, pushing us to outperform and outshine others in order to secure our place in the world.

However, the desire to win extends far beyond physical survival. It evolves into a quest for personal fulfillment, self-actualization, and the realization of our potential. It is an integral part of our pursuit of happiness and a way to measure our progress and growth. Wanting to win becomes a driving force that pushes us to set goals, strive for excellence, and elevate ourselves to new heights.

To truly understand the desire to win, we must explore its intricacies. One aspect is the innate competitive spirit present within us. Competition is embedded in human nature, driving us to test our limits, challenge ourselves, and inch closer to victory. Whether it is in sports, academics, or professional endeavors, the desire to win pushes us to reach our highest potential.

The desire to win manifests differently in everyone. It can stem from various sources such as personal ambition, a need for validation, or a desire for recognition and acclaim. Each person's motivations are unique and influenced by their upbringing, values, and experiences. But irrespective of the underlying motivation, the desire to win acts as a powerful catalyst that propels us forward.

Wanting to win is a mindset that goes beyond the external trappings of success. True winners understand that winning is not just about the result but also the process. It is about embracing the journey, learning from failures, and continuously improving. The desire to win creates a growth-oriented mindset, where individuals see challenges as opportunities and setbacks as valuable lessons.

Additionally, the desire to win is intertwined with our need for self-expression and validation. Achievements allow us to prove our worth, validate our abilities, and gain recognition from others. In a world that often measures success through tangible outcomes, the desire to win becomes a means of establishing our value in society. It is essential to differentiate between external validation and intrinsic motivation. True winners draw strength from within, relying on their sense of satisfaction and fulfillment rather than seeking validation solely from external sources.

The desire to win can have profound effects on our emotional well-being. Accomplishing our goals and experiencing the thrill of victory can evoke feelings of euphoria boosting our self-confidence and self-esteem. It is vital to strike a balance and not become overly fixated on external validation. The desire to win should be grounded in self-awareness and a genuine passion for growth rather than a constant craving for external approval.

In the pursuit of victory, it is crucial to maintain ethical principles and integrity. Winning at any cost is a hollow victory that leaves a bitter aftertaste. True winners understand the importance of fair play, respect for their opponents, and upholding moral values. They recognize that true success is measured not just by triumphs, but also by the positive impact they create in the world and the lives of those around them.

The desire to win also transcends individual pursuits and can be harnessed to create positive change on a larger scale. In collective endeavors, such as team sports, community projects, or shared goals within organizations, the desire to win becomes a unifying force. It fosters collaboration, cooperation, and constructive interaction, enabling groups to achieve extraordinary outcomes that surpass individual capabilities. The pursuit of victory becomes a shared journey, where each member contributes their unique strengths to achieve a common goal.

Ultimately, the desire to win is deeply personal. It represents the pursuit of excellence, the continuous striving for growth, and the unwavering commitment to self-improvement. It encompasses our dreams, aspirations, and the belief that we can achieve greatness. The desire to win propels us forward, fuels our perseverance, and encourages us to push beyond our limits, unveiling our true potential.

Wanting to win is a fundamental aspect of human nature. It encompasses our desires for fulfillment, self-actualization, and growth. It drives us to test our limits, challenge ourselves, and strive for greatness. The desire to win is a multifaceted and complex force, shaped by individual motivations, values, and experiences. It is through this desire that we explore the depths of our potential, carve our path toward success, and leave an indelible mark on the world.

35

MAKE IT HAPPEN, SHOCK EVERYONE

In this chapter, we delve into the power of pushing beyond your limits and completely surpassing the expectations of those around you. It is about defying societal norms and preconceived notions, not just for others, but for yourself as well.

To "make it happen" means taking charge of your aspirations and dreams, fueling them with unwavering determination and an unshakeable belief in yourself. It is about setting audacious goals, ones that seem impossible, and then embarking on a transformative journey to achieve them. But it goes beyond mere goal setting; it is about defying the odds and breaking through the barriers that society and even your self-doubt have placed before you.

When you embark on this path, you can shock everyone, to leave them astounded and inspired. It is in those moments when you go beyond what is expected that you prove your true potential. It is about showing the world that limitations are nothing more than illusions, waiting to be shattered.

Shocking everyone is not about seeking validation or impressing others; it is about proving to yourself that you have what it takes to achieve greatness. By pushing the boundaries of what is possible and embracing discomfort, you unleash a power within you that is unstoppable. It is about tapping into the deep reservoirs of courage and resilience that lie within, paving your own path and redefining what is considered attainable.

To shock everyone, you must begin by cultivating an unshakable belief in yourself and your abilities. Confidence is the key that unlocks the doors to extraordinary achievements. As the renowned novelist and poet Oscar Wilde once said, "To love oneself is the beginning of a lifelong romance."

Building confidence is not a one-time endeavor; it is a continuous process. It requires nurturing and self-reflection. Understand that self-doubt will arise, but do not let it overpower your conviction. Practice positive affirmations, surround yourself with a supportive network, and actively challenge the negative thoughts that try to hold you back. Embrace every opportunity to build your confidence, knowing that it is the foundation upon which exceptional accomplishments are built.

With self-belief as your guiding light, you must dare to dream fearlessly. Embrace ambitions that intimidate you, for they hold the potential for immense transformation. Disregard the whispers of doubt and disbelief, lest they quell the fire of your aspirations. Instead, fuel your dreams with conviction, nourish them with relentless determination, and watch as they grow into magnificent realities.

Shocking everyone also necessitates a willingness to step out of your comfort zone. Growth and transformation reside just beyond the borders of familiarity. It is easy to become complacent and settle for what is comfortable, but that is not the path to greatness. Allow yourself to embrace discomfort, for it is within those uncharted territories that greatness awaits. Push yourself to explore new skills, expand your knowledge, and gain diverse perspectives. Embrace challenges as opportunities for growth, knowing that every step taken outside your comfort zone brings you closer to your true potential.

Perseverance is another vital ingredient in the recipe for shocking everyone. The road to success is often fraught with challenges, obstacles, and setbacks. But it is in these moments of adversity that true character is revealed. Embrace failure as a powerful teacher, let it fuel your determination, and forge ahead with renewed vigor. Remember, it is not the number of times you fall but rather the number of times you rise that truly counts.

Cultivate resilience and tenacity by shifting your mindset towards adversity. Instead of viewing obstacles as roadblocks, see them as avenues to growth. Develop the ability to adapt and bounce back from setbacks, fueling your determination to overcome them. Embrace the spirit of never giving up and channel your energy into finding creative solutions, accepting feedback as a tool for improvement, and continuously learning from your experiences.

Making it happen and shocking everyone requires a level of dedication and discipline that goes beyond the ordinary. Success does not come easily or overnight; it requires consistent effort and a commitment to excellence. It is in the countless hours of deliberate practice, the relentless pursuit of knowledge, and the cultivation of discipline that true mastery emerges. Embrace the process, relish the small victories along the way, and let them nourish your journey.

Invest in your personal growth by seeking out mentors, role models, and opportunities to expand your skill set. Surround yourself with a community of ambitious individuals who share your passion for greatness. Collaboration and learning from the wisdom of others can exponentially amplify your progress.

The journey of making it happen and shocking everyone is not solely about the result; it is about the person you become along the way. It teaches you resilience, patience, and perseverance. It molds you into a stronger, wiser, and more adaptable individual. Embrace the inner transformation that occurs as you strive to exceed expectations, for it is often the most significant reward of all.

By embracing the power within you, defying societal expectations, and persisting in the face of adversity, you can make it happen and shock everyone. Break free from the shackles of conformity and redefine what is possible. In doing so, not only will you inspire others to reach for the extraordinary, but you will also elevate humanity by showing that limitations are but temporary illusions, waiting to be shattered. Your journey towards greatness will not only change your life but also leave an indelible mark on the world.

36

CHASE YOUR DREAMS WITH RELENTLESS DETERMINATION

In a world filled with challenges and uncertainties, chasing our dreams requires a relentless determination that fuels our journey. It is this unwavering spirit that sets apart those who achieve greatness from those who settle for mediocrity. When faced with obstacles along the path, it is easy to be discouraged and lose sight of our aspirations. However, those who possess a steadfast resolve are the ones who rise above adversity and embrace their true potential.

Chasing your dreams with relentless determination means refusing to let circumstances define your destiny. It means unwaveringly believing in your abilities and staying focused on your goals, regardless of the external forces that may try to sway you off course. It requires cultivating a mindset that embraces challenges as opportunities for growth and self-discovery as a guide on the path to success.

To nurture this drive, it is essential to develop a clear and well-defined vision of what you want to achieve. Set SMART goals—specific, measurable, attainable, relevant, and time-bound objectives—that provide a roadmap for your journey. Having a clear direction allows you to break down the daunting pursuit into manageable steps, making the path to success appear less overwhelming.

Relentless determination necessitates courage—the courage to take risks, to step out of your comfort zone, and to face the fear of failure head-on. It is in the face of uncertainty that true growth occurs, and new opportunities manifest. Embracing the unknown, though daunting, carries the potential for unimaginable rewards.

Maintaining unwavering determination is not without its difficulties. Doubts and self-questioning may creep in, making you question whether your dreams are attainable or if you possess the necessary skills and abilities. In these moments, it is crucial to dig deep within yourself, summoning the inner strength to push forward. Look to your role models and mentors who have faced similar challenges, drawing inspiration from their journey, and understanding that greatness often emerges from the darkest moments.

Surrounding yourself with a support system is paramount. Seek out individuals who believe in you and share your passion. Connect with like-minded souls who understand the challenges you face and can provide support and inspiration along the way. These individuals will serve as pillars of strength when you need to lean on somebody or provide the gentle nudge that propels you forward during moments of doubt.

While relentless determination is a driving force, it is essential to balance it with self-care. Taking care of your physical, mental, and emotional well-being is crucial to sustaining your energy and focus. Incorporate practices such as exercise, mindfulness, and self-reflection into your routine to nurture a sense of balance and prevent burnout. Remember that self-care is not a selfish act; it is a necessary investment in your long-term success.

In the pursuit of your dreams, it is important to acknowledge that failure is an inevitable part of the journey. Setbacks and disappointments do not define you or your abilities but rather offer valuable lessons. Embrace failures as opportunities to learn, grow, and refine your approach. Resilience becomes a companion, pushing you forward and enabling you to adapt and evolve in the face of adversity.

Measure your progress not only by the results but also by the person you have become throughout the journey. Embrace personal growth and transformation as integral parts of chasing your dreams. Discover the strengths you did not know you possessed, learn from your mistakes, and celebrate the small victories and milestones that signify your unwavering commitment and progress.

Ultimately, chasing your dreams with relentless determination is about more than achieving a specific outcome. It is about the pursuit of authenticity, passion, and purpose. It is about embracing discomfort and stepping outside your comfort zone, for it is in those moments of vulnerability that true magic happens. The journey toward your dreams is an opportunity for self-discovery, an expedition through which you uncover your true potential and leave a lasting impact on the world.

Remember, your dreams are worth fighting for. Embrace the challenges, setbacks, and doubts as mere fuel on your path to success. With unwavering determination and a belief in yourself, you can conquer any obstacle standing in your way. The world awaits a masterpiece only you can create—so let your relentless determination ignite the spark of your greatness.

37

STRIVE FOR PROGRESS, NOT PERFECTION

In a world that often glorifies perfection, it is important to remember that striving for progress is what truly matters. Perfection is an elusive notion, an unattainable standard that can leave us feeling discouraged and inadequate. The pursuit of perfection can consume us, overshadowing our accomplishments and breeding self-doubt. Instead of fixating on attaining the unattainable, we must shift our focus towards progress – a mindset that acknowledges our imperfections yet empowers us to embrace growth and continuous improvement.

The pursuit of progress is not a linear path, but rather a dynamic journey filled with opportunities for personal and professional development. It is a constant quest to discover our potential, to challenge our limits, and to make positive changes in our lives. When we strive for progress, we reject the status quo and become agents of our own transformation.

One of the fundamental aspects of progress is the willingness to take risks and step out of our comfort zones. By venturing into the unknown, we expose ourselves to new experiences, ideas, and perspectives. We become more adaptable and open-minded, expanding our horizon, and broadening our understanding of the world. It is through these bold leaps that we unearth hidden talents, unlock untapped creativity, and discover our true passions.

Embracing progress requires an understanding that it is not without its challenges. It demands perseverance and resilience in the face of setbacks and failures. It is important to remember that progress does not occur without hurdles. These setbacks are not signs of defeat or inadequacy; instead, they are valuable opportunities for growth and learning. Each setback offers lessons that shape our character, strengthen our resolve, and fortify our resilience. By reframing failure as feedback, we shift our mindset and approach challenges with determination and optimism. It is in these moments of adversity that we develop the grit necessary to overcome obstacles and forge our way forward.

Striving for progress also means recognizing that comparison is a fruitless endeavor. Every individual's journey is unique with its own twists, turns, and pace. It is counterproductive to measure our progress against someone else's because we are all on different paths. Our focus should instead be on our personal growth and improvement, celebrating our own achievements and milestones, no matter how small they may seem. By redirecting our energy towards self-reflection and self-compassion, we create an environment that nurtures our progress.

In the pursuit of progress, we cultivate a growth mindset – the belief that our abilities and intelligence can be developed through dedication and hard work. This mindset allows us to embrace challenges as opportunities for growth, rather than as insurmountable obstacles. We become more resilient and persistent, knowing that setbacks are temporary and do not define our ultimate potential. With a growth mindset, we become lifelong learners, continuously seeking new knowledge, skills, and experiences that propel us further along our journey.

Striving for progress means appreciating the process as much as the outcome. While attainment of goals and achievements is fulfilling, it is the journey itself that shapes us, deepens our understanding of ourselves, and offers moments of profound growth and self-discovery. This journey, filled with its ebbs and flows, becomes the tapestry of our lives – a testament to our resilience, determination, and desire for continuous improvement.

As we embrace progress, we must also remember to celebrate the small victories along the way. It is through acknowledging our progress, no matter how incremental it may be, that we find the motivation and inspiration to keep moving forward. Each step forward, no matter how small, is a testament to our dedication and resilience. By recognizing and acknowledging our progress, we fuel our motivation and cultivate a sense of accomplishment, further propelling us towards our goals.

In our pursuit of progress, we must also cultivate patience and self-compassion. Rome was not built in a day, and neither is progress achieved overnight. It takes time and consistency to make meaningful changes in our lives. It is important to set realistic expectations and to show ourselves kindness and understanding throughout the process. We must remember that progress is not a race; it is a lifelong journey, a continuous cycle of growth and improvement.

So, let go of the idea of perfection and embrace the infinite possibilities of progress. Celebrate each step forward, no matter how small, and acknowledge that setbacks are simply detours, not roadblocks. Embrace challenges as opportunities for growth and honor the uniqueness of your own journey. With a growth mindset and an unwavering commitment to progress, you will unlock your true potential and revel in the magnificent journey called life.

38

SWEAT, SACRIFICE, AND SUCCESS

In the pursuit of success, there are no shortcuts or easy paths. It requires an almost indispensable commitment and an unwavering determination to give it your all. These three interwoven elements form the very fabric of achieving greatness in any endeavor.

Let us dive deeper into each of these components to understand their significance in the glorious journey toward success.

Sweat, the physical manifestation of hard work, serves as the cornerstone of achieving greatness. It represents the long hours spent honing one's craft, pushing physical and mental limits, and challenging oneself beyond perceived capabilities. Sweat is the embodiment of dedication, discipline, and perseverance.

When we choose to embrace sweat, we are making a conscious decision to transform mere aspirations into tangible achievements. It symbolizes an unwavering commitment to prioritize our goals, rolling up our sleeves, and putting in the legwork required to ascend to new heights. Sweat binds us to our dreams - the evidence of our unwavering determination etched on our brows.

But sweat alone is not enough. It must be accompanied by sacrifice, the noble act of relinquishing immediate gratification in exchange for long-term gains. Sacrifice requires us to let go of comfort and familiarity, making tough choices that align with our goals. It is about channeling our energies toward what truly matters, embracing delayed gratification, and recognizing the worth of investing in our potential.

Sacrifice demands prioritizing personal growth over fleeting desires, acknowledging that the road to success is often paved with difficult decisions and forsaken pleasures. It empowers us to transcend the boundaries of our comfort zones and venture into uncharted territories. Sacrifice enables us to create space in our lives for the pursuit of greatness, making room for the necessary work, study, and self-reflection that propels us closer to our goals.

However, sweat and sacrifice alone cannot guarantee success. Without the right mindset, the foundation crumbles, and the journey becomes arduous. The mindset required for greatness is one of focus, resilience, and adaptability. It is a belief in our capabilities and an unwavering confidence in our ability to overcome the obstacles that lie in our path.

Success is not a linear journey but a tumultuous adventure. It is a symphony of victories and defeats, triumphs, and setbacks. During moments of doubt and failure, it is our mindset that becomes our compass, guiding us back on course and propelling us forward. It is through learning from our mistakes, picking ourselves up, and persisting in the face of adversity that we forge the character and resilience required for true success.

Embracing the right mindset means cultivating self-awareness and a growth mindset, understanding that failure is not a measure of our worth but an opportunity for growth and improvement. It involves maintaining focus amidst distractions, adapting to changing circumstances, and seeking continuous learning and self-improvement. A resilient mindset enables us to bounce back from setbacks, rise above challenges, and seize the opportunities that arise along the way.

In the grand tapestry of greatness, sweat, sacrifice, and success are inextricably entwined, each amplifying the other. They form the building blocks upon which our destinies are shaped. The pursuit of success demands nothing less than the full dedication of our physical and mental faculties, the willingness to make difficult choices, and a mindset that endures through the highs and lows of the journey.

Remember, the path to greatness is not for the faint of heart, but it is through the embodiment of sweat, sacrifice, and the right mindset that triumph and fulfillment are brought within our grasp.

39

THE GREATEST GLORY IN LIVING LIES NOT IN FALLING,

BUT IN RISING EVERY TIME WE FALL

Life, with all its intricacies and complexities, is a constant dance of triumphs and tribulations. Within its embrace, we encounter unforeseen challenges, experience heartache, and stumble upon moments that test the very fibers of our being. It is in these moments of falling, both literal and metaphorical, that we are allowed—an opportunity to rise, transcend our limitations, and discover the depths of our strength.

To rise every time, we must create a symphony of resilience, a masterpiece woven from the threads of determination, and unwavering belief in oneself. It requires summoning the courage to confront our fears, to face adversity head-on, and to refuse to be confined by the limitations imposed upon us.

But rising after a fall is not an easy journey. It is marked by an intricate tapestry of emotions, where triumph and despair intertwine in a delicate dance. In the moments of darkness, when despair threatens to consume us, it is vital to find solace in the knowledge that within every fall lies the potential for growth, learning, and self-discovery.

Failure, often seen as an indomitable foe, holds within it the seeds of wisdom. It is through the cracks of our failures that the light of self-awareness and personal growth shines through. In these moments, we are allowed to reflect upon our choices, reevaluate our paths, and emerge stronger, wiser, and more resilient.

Rising after a fall requires a willingness to endure discomfort and a commitment to facing our demons. It involves stripping away the layers of ego, accepting responsibility for our actions, and embracing humility. Only by acknowledging our vulnerabilities and learning from our mistakes can we truly rise and move forward with purpose.

But be wary, for the process of rising after a fall is not for the faint of heart. It demands perseverance, resilience, and a relentless pursuit of personal growth. It is a journey of self-discovery that requires patience, as the road to redemption is rarely a swift one.

In these defining moments, it is crucial not to confuse a fall as a reflection of one's worth. The world is often quick to judge, to label failures as permanent markers of identity. Yet, it is within the depths of our falls that we must find the strength to challenge these perceptions and redefine our narratives.

Our ability to rise after a fall is not diminished by the opinions of others, for we are the authors of our own stories. Each fall shapes us, molds us into more resilient beings, and provides us with the tools to face future challenges with a newfound sense of purpose.

To rise every time, we fall is not to deny the pain or hardships we experience. It is an acknowledgment of the inherent power within us—the power to decide how we will respond to adversity, and how we will use our falls as pathways towards greatness.

In this journey of rising after a fall, we are not alone. Our companions are the countless individuals who have risen from the depths of despair, who have triumphed against all odds, and who continue to inspire us with their stories of resilience. It is through their examples that we find solace and motivation to embrace our falls as opportunities for growth and transformation.

Remember, the greatest glory lies not in a life without falls or failures but in our unwavering determination to rise every time. Let us not be disheartened by the falls we encounter, but rather let them be reminders of our strength, our resilience, and our ability to soar to new heights. And, as we rise, let us extend a helping hand to those who may have stumbled along the way, for by supporting others in their journeys, we become part of a cycle of redemption and hope.

In the end, it is not the falls that define us; it is our capacity to rise. With each rise, we paint our masterpieces, fill the pages of our stories with resilience and courage, and leave a legacy for all those who come after us. So, let us continue to rise, passionately and fearlessly, embracing each fall as an opportunity to transcend our limitations and become our greatest selves.

40

VICTORY IS SWEET
WHEN YOU'VE KNOWN DEFEAT

Victory, an elusive and highly coveted prize, has a depth of meaning that transcends mere success. It is a multifaceted gem with surfaces that shimmer in different shades, reflecting the complexity of the human experience. To truly understand the profound nature of victory, one must delve deeper, exploring the myriad layers that encompass its essence.

Within the tapestry of life, victory emerges as a divine alchemy born from the crucible of struggle. It is an amalgamation of resilience, perseverance, and unyielding determination. It is a testament to the extraordinary capacity of the human spirit to rise above adversity, transforming failure into fuel for growth and progress.

The journey towards victory is rarely a linear path, but rather a tumultuous voyage through uncharted waters. It is marked by countless setbacks, disappointments, and moments of doubt. In these moments of darkness, when all seems lost, one must summon the strength to forge ahead, defying the siren call of surrender.

It is in the face of defeat that character is forged, honed, and polished. The weight of failure bears down on the weary soul, testing its mettle and resilience. The bitter taste of defeat lingers, saturating every thought and emotion, but it is in these very depths that seeds of greatness are sown.

For it is within failure that we are impelled to introspection, compelled to examine the intricate tapestry of our strengths and weaknesses. It demands self-reflection and forces us to confront our flaws and limitations. This often-painful process illuminates the path towards growth and self-improvement, propelling us forward with newfound clarity.

Victory is not haphazardly bestowed upon the fortunate few; it is earned through tireless effort, unwavering commitment, and an unquenchable thirst for progress. Each victory carries within it the collective wisdom of the past, the culmination of lessons learned from countless failures and near-misses. It is the result of relentless determination and the courage to persist, even when the odds are stacked against us.

Furthermore, victory is not an individual conquest but a collective achievement. It is strengthened by the support, guidance, and encouragement of those around us. The interconnectedness of human existence amplifies the significance of shared victories, underscored by the bonds formed through mutual struggle and triumph.

In the pursuit of victory, we often discover that success is not merely a destination but a transformative process. It is an ever-evolving journey, characterized by adaptability, resilience, and continuous growth. The pursuit of victory transcends the realms of achievement and recognition; it becomes a lifelong mission to unlock our truest potential and make a positive impact on the world around us.

But victory, even after tasting the depths of defeat, is not without its complexities. The passing nature of triumph demands humility and vigilance. It urges us not to rest on our laurels, but to remain vigilant, embracing the inevitable challenges that lie ahead. For true victory lies not in a single milestone, but in the relentless pursuit of excellence, innovation, and leaving a lasting legacy.

So, dear reader, as you navigate your own journey, let the taste of victory linger on your tongue. Embrace the depth of its meaning and savor its complexity. Allow the lessons learned from the depths of defeat to shape your perspective and fuel your unwavering resolve. With each step forward, remember that victory is not merely an external conquest; it is an internal transformation, a testament to the unyielding indomitable spirit that resides within us all.

41

STAY FOCUSED AND NEVER LOSE SIGHT OF YOUR GOALS

In the journey towards success, one of the most crucial attributes that separates winners from the rest is an unwavering focus and an unyielding commitment to their goals. It is easy to get distracted by the noise and chaos of everyday life, but champions understand the importance of staying focused on what truly matters.

When you have a clear vision of your goals and dreams, it becomes easier to filter out distractions and stay on track. However, staying focused is not always easy. It requires discipline, self-control, and the ability to prioritize your time and energy effectively.

One way to enhance your focus and productivity is by setting specific, measurable, achievable, relevant, and time-bound (SMART) goals. When your goals are well-defined, it is easier to break them down into smaller, actionable steps that you can work on consistently. By having a clear roadmap, you can direct your efforts towards the tasks that will bring you closer to your desired outcome.

Staying focused requires developing a mindset that refuses to settle for mediocrity. It means constantly pushing yourself outside of your comfort zone and embracing challenges as opportunities for growth. Remember, some of the greatest achievements in history were accomplished by individuals who dared to dream big and refused to be deterred by setbacks or failures.

Another key aspect of staying focused is managing your time and priorities effectively. Learn to differentiate between important tasks and distractions. It is essential to have a system in place to organize your daily activities and allocate time for the most significant tasks that will contribute to your long-term success. This might mean sacrificing short-term gratification for long-term gains.

In addition to managing your time, taking care of your mental and physical well-being is crucial for maintaining focus. It is no secret that a healthy body and mind are fundamental to peak performance. Practice mindfulness and meditation to train your mind to stay present and not get overwhelmed by external pressures. Engage in regular exercise and maintain a healthy lifestyle, as physical well-being directly impacts your cognitive function and focus.

Furthermore, surround yourself with people who support your goals and have a positive influence on your journey. Seek out mentors, coaches, or like-minded individuals who can provide guidance, accountability, and motivation. Remember, success is not achieved in isolation but through the collective effort of a supportive network. Rally together with those who believe in you and your dreams, as their encouragement and inspiration will fuel your determination to stay focused.

Managing distractions is another crucial aspect of staying focused. In today's hyper-connected world, it is easy to fall into the trap of constant notifications, social media scrolling, and other forms of digital distraction. To combat this, create boundaries and establish designated periods of uninterrupted focus. Turn off notifications, set specific times for checking emails and messages, and create a distraction-free environment. By minimizing external distractions, you can immerse yourself fully in the task at hand and optimize your productivity.

Staying focused requires mental resilience and the ability to overcome self-doubt and negative thoughts. Develop a growth mindset that embraces challenges and views failure as a path towards success. Embrace a positive attitude and practice self-affirmation to remind yourself of your capabilities and worthiness in achieving your goals.

Surround yourself with affirmations, visual reminders, or inspirational quotes that reinforce your focus and determination.

Lastly, never lose sight of your goals. Always stay connected to your purpose and the reasons why you started on this path. When challenges arise, remind yourself of the bigger picture and the prize that awaits you at the end. Reflect on the progress you have already made and the obstacles you have overcome. Allow these achievements to boost your confidence and let them be the wind beneath your wings.

Each day is an opportunity to move closer to your dreams. Embrace the journey and the process, for it is through the trials and tribulations that true growth occurs. The path to success may not always be linear, but having unwavering focus will empower you to adapt, learn, and thrive in the face of adversity.

In conclusion, staying focused and never losing sight of your goals is a fundamental aspect of achieving success. It requires discipline, effective time management, managing distractions, and a strong support system. By maintaining clarity, prioritizing your efforts, and staying committed to your dreams, you can overcome obstacles and reach your full potential. So, stay focused, stay determined, and watch your dreams transform into reality.

42

SUCCESS IS A JOURNEY, NOT A DESTINATION

In our fast-paced and highly competitive society, the pursuit of success has become an all-encompassing endeavor for many individuals. We have been conditioned to believe that success is a fixed state of achievement—a moment frozen in time where all our efforts culminate in ultimate triumph. We are bombarded with societal messages that laud immediate results and instant gratification, leading us to believe that success is a linear progression from point A to point B. But the reality is far more profound.

True success knows no boundaries, no time limits, and no fixed parameters. It is an ever-evolving journey that defies conventional notions. It embraces the fluidity of life, constantly pushing us to reinvent ourselves, challenge our comfort zones, and explore uncharted territories. Success is not a destination to be reached, but a continuous process that unfolds over a lifetime.

At the heart of any successful journey lies an intimate understanding of oneself. To truly embark on the path to success, we must dig deep within and take an honest inventory of our passions, values, and aspirations. What drives us? What do we truly want to achieve? These questions lay the foundation for our unique definition of success, guiding our actions and shaping our journey.

Navigating the road to success requires resilience and mental fortitude. It demands a willingness to face adversity head-on, knowing that obstacles are not insurmountable barriers but growth opportunities. It is in moments of hardship and struggle that we forge our character, learn valuable lessons, and develop the inner strength necessary to persevere.

The journey to success is not a solitary one. It is enriched by the relationships we cultivate along the way. Surrounding ourselves with supportive individuals who inspire, challenge, and believe in us is vital to our progress. These connections become anchors of encouragement and provide us with unique perspectives and insights that help shape our trajectory.

Central to this journey is the concept of personal growth. True success extends beyond achieving external accolades; it encompasses an internal transformation of the self. It calls for continuous introspection, self-reflection, and an unwavering commitment to self-improvement. As we confront our fears, break through self-imposed limitations, and embrace vulnerability, we unlock hidden potential and discover facets of ourselves we never knew existed.

To fully embrace the journey to success, we must relinquish our obsession with immediate outcomes. It is imperative to celebrate the small victories, the incremental progress that fuels our motivation and keeps us moving forward. Success can be found in the lessons learned from failure, the perseverance displayed in the face of adversity, and the resilience to get back up again and again.

Success should not be confined to narrow parameters set by society. It encompasses holistic well-being—both physically and mentally. Taking care of our bodies and minds is an essential part of the journey. Nurturing our emotional health, practicing self-care, seeking balance, and cultivating a growth mindset are critical components of sustained success that create a solid foundation for personal fulfillment.

As we engage in this transformative voyage, it is crucial to remember that success is not an end in itself. It is not an endpoint where we can rest on our laurels and bask in our achievements. Instead, success invites us to be lifelong learners, continuously seeking knowledge, improving our skills, and adapting to ever-evolving circumstances.

Ultimately, success is an odyssey of self-discovery and self-actualization. It beckons us to dream big, to aspire to greatness, and to embrace our unique abilities. It is directed not by societal expectations or external validation but by our individual passions, values, and purpose. Success is not a destination; it is the unending journey that shapes us, fuels our growth, and allows us to leave an indelible mark on the world.

So, let us embark on this extraordinary journey with open minds, resilient spirits, and unwavering determination. Let us be guided by our own definition of success, for it is uniquely ours to define and pursue. And let us revel in every moment, cherishing the profound experience of transformation and purpose that comes with embracing the unwavering path to success.

43

YOUR BODY CAN STAND ALMOST ANYTHING,

IT'S YOUR MIND YOU MUST CONVINCE

In the journey towards achieving greatness, we often encounter physical and mental challenges that push us to our limits. While our bodies possess incredible resilience and endurance, it is our mind that often becomes the deciding factor in our success.

Our bodies are marvels of nature, finely tuned machines capable of adapting and transforming to meet various physical demands. They have the remarkable ability to push through pain, endure intense training sessions, grueling workouts, and exhausting competitions. The human body encompasses an intricate system of muscles, bones, and organs, all woven together to support strength, agility, and stamina.

The body's adaptability is highlighted in the stories of exceptional athletes who have defied conventional limitations. From marathon runners who push through the "wall" of physical fatigue to weightlifters who lift staggering amounts of weight. The human body's potential seems boundless. It can withstand rigorous training regimes, overcome injuries, and bounce back from setbacks. The physical capabilities we possess are truly awe-inspiring.

However, as incredible as our bodies may be, it is the boundless power of our minds that holds the key to unlocking our full potential. Our minds, our thoughts, hold the immense power to determine our course of action, shape our attitudes, and dictate our behavior. They can propel us forward or hold us back, depending on the narrative we choose to believe.

The inner voice within our heads is often filled with self-doubt and fear. It whispers that we are not strong enough, not talented enough, or not worthy of the success we seek. This negative dialogue can become a formidable barrier, hindering us from pushing beyond our perceived limits. However, we have the power to change this narrative, to rewrite the script that plays in our minds.

To strengthen our minds, we must embark on an intentional journey of self-discovery and self-improvement. This requires an honest examination of our thoughts, beliefs, and past conditioning. It entails uncovering the root causes of our self-doubt, fears, and limiting beliefs, and challenging them with courage and determination.

Mental resilience is a skill to be honed, just like physical strength. It involves cultivating a mindset that embraces challenges, sees setbacks as opportunities for growth, and views failure as a pathway to success. Developing mental resilience requires practice, discipline, and a commitment to self-growth.

One way to cultivate mental resilience is through the practice of positive affirmations. By consistently repeating positive statements about ourselves and our abilities, we rewire our minds to believe in our potential. We replace self-limiting beliefs with empowering thoughts, rewiring our brains for success.

Another powerful tool is visualization. By vividly imagining ourselves achieving our goals, and experiencing the sensations and emotions that accompany success, we create a mental blueprint for accomplishment. Visualization helps build confidence, as our minds become accustomed to the feelings of success. It also serves as a guidance system, directing our efforts towards our desired outcome.

In addition to affirmations and visualization, finding purpose and aligning our goals with our values deepens our mental fortitude. When our actions are driven by a strong sense of purpose, a belief that what we are doing is meaningful and impactful, we tap into an extra reserve of motivation and determination. Purpose provides a solid foundation that strengthens our resolve in the face of adversity.

Cultivating a growth mindset is essential for mental resilience. Embracing the belief that abilities can be developed through dedication and hard work, rather than being fixed traits, allows us to approach challenges with a sense of curiosity and a desire to grow. Instead of fearing failure, we see setbacks as opportunities to learn and improve. This mindset shift enables us to persevere through obstacles, knowing that each step forward, regardless of the outcome, is progress toward our ultimate goal.

Developing emotional intelligence plays a pivotal role in strengthening our minds. By understanding and managing our emotions effectively, we can navigate challenges and setbacks with greater ease. Emotional intelligence allows us to build resilience, maintain focus, and make informed decisions even in high-pressure situations. It empowers us to stay calm, focused, and determined, regardless of external circumstances.

Engaging in mindfulness and meditation practices can also enhance mental resilience. By training our minds to be present in the moment and observing our thoughts and emotions without judgment, we cultivate a greater sense of clarity and resilience. Mindfulness helps us detach from negative thought patterns and reframe challenges as opportunities for growth. It fosters a calm and centered mindset that enables us to navigate uncertainty and adversity with grace and ease.

While our bodies possess incredible physical potential, it is the power of our minds that holds the key to unlocking it. We must nurture our mental resilience, silence the negative self-talk, and replace it with empowering thoughts. By training our minds to be strong, focused, and resilient, we can transcend physical limitations and accomplish feats that were once deemed impossible. The mind truly is the ultimate force that propels us toward greatness.

44

WINNING STARTS WITH YOUR ATTITUDE

Attitude plays a vital role in determining our success in any endeavor. It sets the tone for our actions, decisions, and overall approach to life. When it comes to winning, having the right attitude is essential.

A winning attitude begins with believing in yourself and your abilities. It is about having unwavering confidence in your skills and talents, knowing deep within that you can achieve great things. This belief serves as the foundation for all your actions and decisions, empowering you to take risks, embrace challenges, and push beyond your comfort zone. Without this firm self-belief, it becomes difficult to overcome obstacles and persevere when the going gets tough.

However, cultivating self-belief is more than just repeating positive affirmations; it requires a deep understanding of your strengths and weaknesses. By truly knowing yourself, you can leverage your talents while continuously improving in areas of growth. This self-awareness allows you to capitalize on your unique set of skills, setting yourself apart from the competition and positioning yourself for success.

Maintaining a positive mindset is another crucial aspect of a winning attitude. It involves embracing a perspective that focuses on solutions rather than problems, seeking opportunities in every situation, and refusing to allow setbacks to derail your progress. It is about training your mind to see difficulties as milestones on your journey, learning experiences that ultimately propel you forward.

A positive attitude not only strengthens your mental resilience but also enhances your overall well-being. It allows you to approach obstacles with a sense of optimism, knowing that you can overcome them. It helps you remain motivated and driven, even in the face of adversity. By adopting a positive mindset, you become a magnetic force, attracting opportunities, and inspiring those around you with your unwavering determination.

In addition to self-belief and a positive outlook, a winning attitude involves taking responsibility for your actions and outcomes. It means accepting that you have control over your choices and that success or failure depends on how you respond to both. Instead of shifting blame onto external factors, a person with a winning attitude looks within and asks themselves how they can improve, learn, and grow. They understand that success lies in their hands and use every experience, both positive and negative, as an opportunity for growth.

Having a winning attitude also means embracing a mindset of continuous learning and improvement. It means being open to feedback, seeking opportunities to expand your knowledge, and constantly honing your skills. A growth mindset allows you to adapt to changing circumstances, keeping you agile and ready to seize new opportunities. With a thirst for knowledge and a commitment to personal development, you position yourself as a lifelong learner, always striving for excellence and pushing the boundaries of your potential.

Furthermore, a winning attitude involves perseverance and resilience. It means not giving up when faced with adversity or failure, but rather learning from those experiences and coming back stronger. A person with a winning attitude understands that setbacks are part of the journey, and that true success often comes after multiple attempts. They view obstacles as opportunities to innovate, to discover new strategies, and to prove their inner strength and determination.

But it is important to remember that a winning attitude is not limited to individual success; it extends to the collective. A winning attitude is contagious. When you embody positivity, confidence, and resilience, it inspires those around you. Your attitude can influence the mindset of others, creating an environment of determination, teamwork, and motivation. A team with a collective winning attitude is more likely to achieve its goals, overcome challenges, and foster a culture of growth and success.

Winning starts with your attitude. It is the foundation upon which success is built. By believing in yourself, maintaining a positive mindset, taking responsibility, embracing continuous learning, and demonstrating perseverance, you set yourself up for victory. Remember, your attitude determines not only your success but also the success of those around you. So, choose to have a winning attitude, and watch the possibilities unfold before you.

45

DON'T WISH FOR IT,
WORK FOR IT

"Don't wish for it, work for it." This pithy quote encapsulates a vital truth – simply wishing for something is passive, while working for it is active. More specifically, working towards your dreams leads to tangible progress and growth, while just wishing for things to be different changes little in your life. There is a massive difference between these two mindsets when it comes to achieving goals and realizing your vision for how you want to live.

We all have things we wish for – more financial freedom, fulfilling relationships, better health, meaningful work. However, as the quote makes clear, simply wishing does very little when it comes to making these desires a reality. It is action, effort, and persistence that actively propels us closer towards the things we care about. Progress does not arise from idle hope; it is forged through work.

What, specifically, does it mean to turn wishes into work? It means breaking down vague dreams into clearly defined, actionable goals. Rather than just wish to start your own company someday, research business models, write a business plan with financial projections, decide on a timeline for getting funding and permits, and so on. Want to own a home? Run the numbers to analyze exactly what you can afford given current finances, consult lenders about mortgage options and credit health, and develop a concrete savings plan that supports your target down payment amount.

Essentially, you need to map out step-by-step plans which allow you to methodically chip away at the overarching dreams you are wishing for. It requires foresight, effort, analytical thinking, and very likely some difficult choices. But dreams wither on the vine if they remain abstract and passive. There is no substitute for doing the work.

And make no mistake – it will not come easy. Any major life goal worth working towards presents challenges which can only be overcome through a commitment to sustained effort. Breaking deeply ingrained habits, learning new skills, sacrificing short-term pleasures for longer-term gain – becoming the type of person who can make your dreams into reality involves some painful growth. Expect failures and setbacks as part of the process. Perseverance emerges from having the fortitude and perspective to see every stumble as a lesson rather than the end of the road.

The work involved certainly goes beyond just effort – work smarter, not only harder. Seek out mentors, study others who have achieved what you aspire to, be strategic in how you spend your time. But while working effectively matters greatly, as the quote tells us, there will never be a shortcut or silver bullet that allows you to simply wish your way to your goals coming true automatically. Any lasting success follows from daily acts of dedication which operationalize your vision into your lived reality, step by step.

At the deepest level, internalizing the fact that sustained effort over the long-haul is the only path forward instills the mindset needed to actualize your potential. The difference between wishing and working is not just semantic – it is the difference between helplessly adrift and intentionally on course towards your chosen destination. Where do you aim to be in 5 years? Wish for it vaguely, or plan it out it in detail and work for it diligently? As the quote makes clear – the choice is yours.

46
SUCCESS IS THE BEST REVENGE

In a world filled with competition, setbacks, and disappointments, the concept of revenge may seem tempting. When faced with adversity, it is natural to want to prove others wrong, to show them that you can achieve greatness despite their doubt or criticism. This desire for revenge can be a powerful motivator, pushing us to work harder and strive for success.

But revenge alone is not enough to sustain us in the long run. It may provide temporary satisfaction, but true fulfillment comes from focusing on our own growth and accomplishments. Success, in its purest form, is the best revenge.

When we channel our energy into improving ourselves, pursuing our dreams, and surpassing our own expectations, we rise above the negativity that others may have imposed upon us. It is in these moments of self-reflection and introspection that we find the strength to reshape our lives and aim for something greater.

Our journey towards success becomes a proclamation of our resilience and tenacity. It is about breaking free from the shackles of doubt and turning adversity into opportunity. Each obstacle becomes a teacher, urging us to push forward and discover the depths of our capabilities.

The path to success can be arduous, filled with countless setbacks and challenges. But it is through these trials that we learn the most valuable lessons. We develop a sense of resilience as we pick ourselves up after each failure, and with each success, we affirm our worthiness for the life we desire.

What sets success as revenge apart from a mere desire for retribution is the transformation that occurs within us. It is about recognizing that our value is not determined by the opinions of others, but rather by our own efforts, determination, and self-belief. Embracing this mindset allows us to liberate ourselves from the burden of seeking validation from external sources.

The pursuit of success as revenge is not fueled by bitterness or a desire to outdo others. It is rooted in our own personal growth and the desire to reach our fullest potential. We have a vision of what we want to achieve, a burning fire within us that propels us forward despite the odds. Along this journey, we cultivate resilience, adaptability, and a deep understanding of ourselves.

In this quest for success, we find mentors who guide us, challenges that mold us, and experiences that shape us. We develop the mindset of a lifelong learner, constantly seeking knowledge and growth in every aspect of our lives. Success becomes a continuous journey, an ever-evolving process of self-discovery and self-mastery.

As we ascend towards our goals, we inspire those around us. Our accomplishments become a beacon of hope for others who aspire to overcome their own obstacles. By displaying our determination, perseverance, and unwavering belief in ourselves, we encourage others to embrace their own power and strive for greatness.

Success, like revenge, has the power to not only transform our own lives but also to create a ripple effect of positive change in the world around us. It is a statement that proclaims our resilience, our ability to transcend adversity, and our unwavering dedication to our dreams.

When we achieve success as a form of revenge, we also challenge the prevailing narratives of limited potential. We defy the societal norms that dictate who we should be and what we can accomplish. We become living proof that anyone, regardless of background or circumstances, can rise above their circumstances and achieve greatness.

Our success serves as a catalyst for inspiration and empowerment. It is a testament to the human spirit's ability to overcome, to adapt, and to thrive. Through our journey towards success, we dismantle the barriers that society sets before us and create a future filled with boundless opportunities for all.

Success as revenge is not about diminishing others or seeking retribution. It is about reclaiming our power, rewriting our narratives, and shaping our own destiny. It is a declaration to the world that no matter what challenges we face, or the doubts others may harbor, we are capable of greatness.

So, let us not be consumed by the desire for revenge. Instead, let us focus on our own growth, pursue our passions with unwavering determination, and use our success as a powerful statement of our capabilities. With each victory we achieve, we defy the doubts, the naysayers, and the haters. Success is the ultimate form of revenge, and it is within our reach if we believe in ourselves and never give up on our dreams.

47

GREAT ATHLETES NEVER STOP LEARNING

You must understand the importance of continuous learning and growth, not just in sports but in all aspects of life. Great athletes embody this mindset, constantly seeking ways to improve their skills and gain a competitive edge.

Athletes who strive for greatness understand that their journey is a never-ending process of learning. They recognize that there is always room for improvement, no matter how talented or accomplished they may be. They embrace the idea that they can always learn something new, whether it is a new technique, strategy, or mental approach.

Learning in sports extends beyond the physical aspects of the game. Great athletes also focus on developing their mental strength and resilience. They study their opponents, analyze their own performances, and identify areas where they can adjust. They seek advice from coaches and mentors, absorbing knowledge and experience that can help them overcome challenges and reach new heights.

To deepen their knowledge and understanding, great athletes often delve into sports psychology, biomechanics, and nutrition, among other fields. They recognize that a comprehensive approach to their development is essential, and they strive to enhance not only their physical skills but also their mental and emotional well-being.

Sports psychology is a discipline that great athletes tap into to gain a mental edge over their competitors. They learn techniques to control their emotions, build confidence, and maintain a focused mindset during high-pressure situations. By understanding the psychological aspects of their sport, they are better equipped to handle adversity and perform at their peak.

Biomechanics, on the other hand, allows athletes to optimize their movements and technique. Through the study of body mechanics and physics, they can refine their movements to maximize efficiency and minimize the risk of injury. By continually analyzing and improving their biomechanics, they can achieve greater speed, power, and precision in their performance.

Nutrition plays a crucial role in an athlete's overall development. Great athletes understand the connection between proper nutrition and optimal performance. They educate themselves on the importance of specific nutrients, timing of meals, and hydration strategies to fuel their bodies effectively. By fueling their bodies with the right nutrients, they can improve their endurance, strength, and recovery, giving them a competitive advantage.

One of the key aspects of being a great athlete is the willingness to step outside of their comfort zone. They actively seek out new experiences and challenges that push their boundaries. They are open to trying different training methods, exploring alternative approaches, and experimenting with new techniques. By doing so, they expand their skill set and gain a deeper understanding of their sport.

Great athletes understand the importance of learning from their past performances. They meticulously analyze game tapes, identifying strengths and weaknesses in their strategies and techniques. They seek feedback from their coaches and teammates, leveraging their insights to make specific adjustments to their game plan. Reflecting on their experiences, they develop a heightened sense of self-awareness and actively work on their weaknesses to turn them into strengths.

Another vital element of continuous learning for athletes is the ability to learn from failure. Great athletes understand that setbacks and losses are part of the journey towards success. Instead of dwelling on their failures, they use them as valuable learning opportunities. They analyze what went wrong, identify areas for improvement, and make the necessary adjustments to come back stronger.

Additionally, great athletes understand the power of collaboration and learning from others. They recognize that everyone has unique strengths and experiences that can be shared and utilized for collective growth. They actively engage with teammates, coaches, and even their competitors to exchange ideas and strategies. By fostering a culture of learning and sharing, they create an environment that enables everyone to thrive and reach their full potential.

Continuous learning and growth are essential for athletes who aspire to greatness. Beyond the physical aspects, they delve into sports psychology, biomechanics, and nutrition to enhance their skills and performance. Stepping out of their comfort zone, learning from past experiences, embracing failure, and engaging with others all contribute to their never-ending journey of improvement. By adopting this mindset, great athletes not only enhance their individual performance but also contribute to the collective growth and success of their team. Just like great athletes, embracing a continuous learning mindset in writing and all areas of life is crucial for achieving greatness.

48

EMBRACE THE PAIN,
AND LET IT FUEL YOUR PASSION

Pain, as intrinsic as it is to human experience, is often viewed as something to be avoided or suppressed. Society has conditioned us to seek comfort and instant gratification, repressing the discomfort that accompanies growth and transformation. True success and fulfillment lie in embracing pain and allowing it to become our driving force.

In the depths of suffering, we are stripped to our core, our vulnerability exposed. It is during these moments that we confront our deepest fears and insecurities, ultimately gaining a profound understanding of ourselves. Pain becomes a powerful catalyst for self-reflection and self-discovery. It urges us to question who we are, what we truly desire, and how far we are willing to go to achieve it.

When we face pain head-on, we begin to unravel the layers that have masked our true potential. It pushes us beyond the boundaries of our comfort zones, forcing us to confront our limitations and test the extent of our capabilities. Discomfort becomes a rite of passage, an initiation into a world of limitless possibilities. It becomes the crucible in which we forge the strength and resilience required to overcome life's challenges.

Pain sets ablaze a fire within us - a relentless desire to prove to ourselves and the world that we are capable of achieving greatness. It inspires us to take that leap of faith, to embark on a journey of self-improvement and personal growth. It provides the motivation we need to push past our perceived limits and venture into uncharted territory.

Beyond the physical or emotional discomfort lies a hidden treasure trove of lessons. It teaches us resilience, teaching us to rise from the depths of despair and never lose sight of our dreams. Pain exposes our vulnerability and cultivates empathy, enabling us to connect with others on a deeper level, understanding their struggles and offering support.

Embracing pain demands discipline and unwavering commitment. It calls for the courage to persist in the face of adversity, refusing to succumb to the allure of an easy path. It is not a passive acceptance of pain but an active choice to harness its energy and transform it into personal growth.

For it is in those moments of pain that we realize the immense strength dwelling within us - the strength we may have once doubted or overlooked. It is through pain that our character is tested and revealed, and we discover our true inner power. It reveals the resilience that anchors us during the storms of life and the tenacity to triumph over seemingly insurmountable obstacles.

But embracing pain does not mean that we become masochistic creatures, relishing torment. It is not about seeking pain for pain's sake, but rather understanding that it is an integral part of growth and progress. It is about embracing discomfort knowing that on the other side lies personal transformation, wisdom, and fulfillment.

The journey of embracing pain is messy, chaotic, and unpredictable. Like a turbulent storm, it can stir up confusion and doubt, making us question our choices and capabilities. But it is during these storms that we discover our greatest potential. It is in these trying times that we dig deep into the reservoirs of our being and discover untapped reservoirs of courage, determination, and resilience.

When we allow pain to guide us, we tap into a wellspring of creativity. It propels us to craft narratives that capture the complexities of the human condition, to seek truths that lie submerged beneath the surface. Pain gives birth to stories of triumph over adversity, unearths deep emotional resonance, and ignites thought-provoking discussions.

Embracing pain is not for the faint-hearted but for those who dare to live life to the fullest. It is a call to confront our fears and embrace the discomfort that arises from pursuing our dreams. Pain, rather than a hindrance, becomes an essential catalyst on the path to greatness. It is in the crucible of painful moments that we forge the foundation of our legacy, leaving an indelible mark on the world.

So, let us boldly step forward, into the unknown, and embrace the pain that accompanies the journey. Let us savor the discomfort, for it is through it that we become more resilient, more compassionate, and more alive. Embrace the pain, and let it be the driving force that propels you towards the heights of your true potential.

49

THE GREATEST GLORY IS NOT IN NEVER FALLING,

BUT RISING EVERY TIME WE FALL

Life is a journey of constant growth and self-discovery. Along this path, we encounter triumphs and failures, joy and heartbreak, success, and disappointment. It is during our lowest moments that we truly discover our strength and resilience, for it is in these moments that we are truly tested.

Failure is not inherently negative; it is a natural part of the human experience. It is through failure that we learn valuable lessons about ourselves and the world around us. Our most significant achievements often arise from navigating through the darkness of setbacks and disappointments. When we stumble, we have the opportunity to rise and reach higher than before.

Embracing failure and learning to rise from it is not an easy task. Our society often emphasizes perfection and success, which can create an aversion to failure. We are conditioned to fear failure, seeing it as a sign of weakness or incompetence. In reality, failure is a pivotal catalyst for personal and professional growth.

To rise from failure requires a shift in perspective. It demands humility and self-reflection. We must learn to view failure as a teacher rather than an adversary – a profound source of wisdom and insight. Every stumble allows us to refine our approach, reassess our goals, and gain a clearer understanding of what truly inspires and drives us.

The journey of rising from failure begins with acknowledging and accepting our mistakes, shortcomings, and missteps. It involves taking a step back, analyzing the situation objectively, and humbly recognizing our role in the outcome. We must resist the temptation to place blame on external factors and instead take responsibility for our part in the experience.

The next crucial step is to learn from our failures. Look closely at what went wrong and critically evaluate our choices and actions. This process requires honesty and vulnerability. It may involve seeking feedback from others and actively listening to their perspectives. By understanding the reasons behind our failures, we gain knowledge and insights that will inform our future Decisions.

It is important to cultivate resilience in the face of failure. Resilience is our ability to bounce back from challenging situations, to adapt and recover. Building resilience can be achieved through various practices such as maintaining a positive mindset, nurturing supportive relationships, and engaging in self-care. Resilience allows us to face failure with courage and determination, knowing that setbacks do not define us but can instead serve as catalysts for growth.

Additionally, failing forward involves learning to embrace vulnerability and taking calculated risks. It means stepping outside our comfort zones and being open to the possibility of failure. When we take risks, we expose ourselves to the potential for both success and failure. However, it is through these risks that we open ourselves up to immense growth and transformation. As the saying goes, "You miss 100% of the shots you don't take." So, we must be willing to take those shots, regardless of the outcome.

Importantly, rising from failure also requires us to practice self-compassion and forgiveness. It is crucial to treat ourselves with kindness and understanding, recognizing that failure is a universal experience. We are often our harshest critics, holding ourselves to impossibly high standards. By extending compassion to ourselves, we create a space for healing and growth. We acknowledge that failure is not a reflection of our worth as individuals, but rather an opportunity for learning and improvement.

The process of rising from failure is not a solitary journey. It is essential to surround ourselves with a strong support system - individuals who believe in us and our dreams. These individuals offer encouragement, guidance, and a safe space for us to share our experiences. Their support helps us persevere and find the strength to rise again, even in the face of adversity.

Failure does not signify the end, but rather a valuable opportunity on the path to achieving success. It is through failure that we learn valuable lessons, discover our resilience, and realize our true potential. Every stumble allows us to rise higher, stronger, and more determined than before. Embrace failure, for it is in our ability to rise every time we fall that our true greatness lies.

50

HARD WORK IS THE PRICE WE MUST PAY FOR SUCCESS

Success is not something that comes easily or by luck. It requires dedication, persistence, and most importantly, hard work. Hard work is the price we must pay for success, and it is through our efforts and determination that we can achieve our goals.

When we look at successful individuals, whether they are athletes, entrepreneurs, or artists, we often only see the end result of their hard work. We see the trophies, the businesses, or the masterpieces they have created. What we do not see is the countless hours they have put in behind the scenes, the sacrifices they have made, and the challenges they have overcome.

Hard work is not a singular event; it is a continuous and ongoing process. It involves setting clear goals and having the discipline to work towards achieving them day in and day out. It means showing up consistently, even when we do not feel motivated or inspired. It means pushing through difficult moments and persevering when faced with obstacles.

The journey to success is not a linear path; it is filled with ups and downs, failures, and successes. Hard work allows us to learn from these experiences and grow stronger. It teaches us the value of resilience, adaptability, and perseverance. It develops our problem-solving skills and helps us develop a proactive and forward-thinking mindset.

Hard work is about more than just putting in long hours or physical labor; it is about working smarter and making the most of our time and resources. It is about setting priorities, managing our time effectively, and focusing on tasks that truly make a difference. It involves constantly seeking knowledge, learning new skills, and staying open to feedback and constructive criticism.

In the pursuit of success, hard work also requires sacrificing short-term pleasures for long-term gains. It means saying no to distractions, temptations, and instant gratification. It involves making tough decisions, prioritizing our goals, and staying committed even when the going gets tough.

Hard work is often accompanied by failure and setbacks. We may encounter obstacles that seem insurmountable, face rejection, or experience periods of self-doubt. In these moments we must dig deep, find strength within ourselves, and keep moving forward. Through these challenges we develop resilience, determination, and the ability to bounce back stronger than ever.

While hard work is essential, it is also important to find balance. Burnout can easily happen if we neglect self-care and neglect other aspects of our lives. Taking breaks, focusing on our physical and mental well-being, and nurturing relationships are crucial for maintaining a healthy and fulfilling life.

The price of success may be high, but the rewards are even greater. When we achieve our goals through hard work, it brings a profound sense of accomplishment and satisfaction that cannot be matched. We appreciate the journey and the effort it took to get there, and the success becomes even sweeter because of the sacrifices we made.

Hard work is not just a means to an end; it is a way of life. It builds character, shapes our values, and molds us into the best versions of ourselves. It teaches us discipline, perseverance, and the importance of embracing challenges. It allows us to unlock our full potential and create a life of purpose and fulfillment.

Beyond the tangible rewards, hard work instills in us a sense of purpose and meaning. It fuels our passion and gives us a sense of direction. When we pour ourselves into our endeavors, whether it is a career, a hobby, or a personal project, we create a sense of fulfillment that goes far beyond external measures of success. Fulfilment lies in knowing that we have given our all and left a lasting impact on the world around us.

In the pursuit of success, hard work also brings us closer to self-discovery. It enables us to explore our strengths and weaknesses, uncover hidden talents, and discover new aspects of ourselves. Through putting in the effort and embracing challenges, we push past our limits, shatter barriers, and unlock our true potential. It is through our hard work that we unearth the essence of who we are and what we are truly capable of achieving.

Additionally, hard work cultivates a growth mindset. It allows us to continuously learn and evolve. With each hurdle we overcome each goal we achieve, we see that our potential is not fixed but expandable. Hard work empowers us to break free from self-imposed limitations and embrace a life of constant growth and improvement. We become lifelong learners, always seeking knowledge, and always pushing ourselves to reach new heights.

Hard work is not meant to be a solitary journey. It requires collaboration, teamwork, and the support of others. Surrounding ourselves with like-minded individuals who share our drive and ambition can be immensely beneficial. They provide motivation, guidance, and a sense of community. Together, we can bolster each other's efforts, celebrate wins, and navigate challenges. The camaraderie that emerges from collective hard work takes success to a whole new level.

Hard work is indeed the price we must pay for success. It goes far beyond the surface-level notion of putting in long hours or physical labor. Hard work encompasses discipline, perseverance, sacrifice, resilience, and self-discovery. It is a transformative journey that shapes us into the best versions of ourselves and enables us to unlock our true potential. So, roll up your sleeves, embrace the challenges, and put in the work. The rewards will surely be worth it in the end.

51

YOU ARE YOUR ONLY LIMIT

In the grand tapestry of life, we often find ourselves entangled in a web of self-imposed limitations. We become trapped within the confines of our own minds, constantly seeking external factors to blame for our perceived failures and limitations. But in truth, the greatest obstacle we face on our journey to success is none other than ourselves.

We have a remarkable knack for underestimating our own worth and potential. We doubt our abilities, question our talents, and allow fear to dictate the boundaries in which we operate. We limit ourselves, convinced that the paths to greatness are reserved for others, that we are unworthy or incapable of reaching such heights.

Yet, if only we could recognize the immense power that lies dormant within us. If only we could grasp the truth that we possess the potential to conquer any obstacle, to soar beyond the limitations we have placed upon ourselves. Within the depths of our being, there exists an untapped well of strength, resilience, and courage waiting to be unleashed.

The first step toward true liberation and self-actualization is to cultivate an unshakable belief in ourselves. We must learn to trust in our capabilities, reaffirm our worth, and acknowledge that we are deserving of success. It is through this profound self-belief that we can shatter the glass ceilings we have constructed and transcend the boundaries that thwart our progress.

But it is not enough to simply believe in our potential. We must be willing to travel uncharted paths, to venture into unfamiliar territories, and to embrace the discomfort that comes with growth. The boundaries of our comfort zones can act as hindrances, thwarting our progress and preventing us from reaching our true potential. By challenging ourselves, stepping into the unknown, and seizing opportunities, we unlock new realms of possibility.

It would be remiss not to acknowledge the difficulties that may arise along the way. Life has a way of throwing unexpected curveballs, undermining our best-laid plans, and testing the fortitude of our spirit. No matter how diligently we work towards our dreams, setbacks and obstacles are inevitable. It is during these moments of adversity that our true mettle is revealed.

During these trying times, we must learn to view failure as a steppingstone rather than a stumbling block. Failure is not a damning verdict on our abilities nor a reflection of our worth. It is merely an opportunity to reassess, recalibrate, and redirect our efforts. Every stumble, setback, or disappointment offers us invaluable lessons, opportunities for growth, and wisdom that can only be gleaned through experiences. We must learn to view failure as a humble teacher, not as a harsh judge.

As we embark upon this transformative quest, we must also be mindful of the company we keep. The people who surround us have a profound impact on our mindset, beliefs, and aspirations. Thus, it becomes imperative to cultivate a tribe of individuals who inspire, uplift, and support us. Seek out those who believe in your innate potential, encourage your dreams, and challenge you to persevere and aim higher.

Surrounding ourselves with individuals who align with our goals and aspirations fosters an environment of growth and empowerment. Together, we can motivate and inspire one another, tapping into the collective wisdom and strength that propels us forward. We must cultivate a community of dreamers, achievers, and visionaries who fuel our passion and remind us that anything is possible.

Ultimately, we must liberate ourselves from the chains of self-doubt and fear. We must liberate ourselves from the confines of our self-imposed limitations. The journey towards greatness is not a culmination but an ongoing process, an ever-evolving ascent towards self-discovery and personal growth. Embrace the boundless potential that resides within you, the unquenchable spirit that yearns to rise above mediocrity.

Cast aside the shackles of self-doubt, for they are self-imposed and fleeting. Embrace the vast expanse of your capabilities, wielding determination, perseverance, and an unwavering belief in yourself. Remember that failure does not define you; it is merely a steppingstone elevating you towards success.

There are no limits to what you can achieve, for you, and only you are the author of your own destiny. You are your only limit, and with every step forward, you pave the way for extraordinary triumphs. So, step boldly into the unknown, trust in your abilities, and let your unyielding belief in yourself be your guiding light. The world awaits your brilliance, your unique contribution, for you possess the power to transcend all limitations and create a life that exceeds your wildest dreams.

52

VICTORY IS EARNED, NOT GIVEN

In the world of champions, victory is not handed out on a silver platter. It is not something that can be bought or given as a gift. Victory is earned through hard work, dedication, and perseverance.

Those who achieve greatness understand that success does not come easy. It is the result of countless hours spent honing their skills, pushing their limits, and overcoming obstacles. It is a culmination of their passion, their commitment, and their unwavering belief in themselves.

To earn victory, one must possess a relentless drive to succeed. It requires a mindset that refuses to accept defeat and that embraces failure as an opportunity for growth. Champions understand that failure is not a reflection of their abilities but an indication of areas that require improvement. It is the willingness to learn from mistakes and adapt their approach that sets them apart.

Determination is a key ingredient in the pursuit of victory. It is the unwavering commitment to a goal, no matter how challenging or distant it may seem. Champions understand that success is not an overnight phenomenon but a journey of perseverance. They embrace the long, arduous path, knowing that every step taken brings them closer to their aspirations.

When setbacks occur, champions do not dwell on them. They understand that failure is not the end but a valuable learning experience. It is through these hardships that character is built, resilience is strengthened, and a deeper understanding of oneself is attained.

True champions celebrate the small victories along the way, acknowledging the progress made, and finding motivation in each triumph, no matter how small. They break their ultimate goal into smaller, more manageable milestones, creating a sense of momentum and accomplishment. By recognizing the incremental achievements, they maintain the fire within them, propelling them forward towards the ultimate victory.

To earn victory, one must embrace discipline. It means making tough choices between immediate gratification and long-term success. Champions understand the sacrifices required for greatness. They willingly forego temporary pleasures, late nights, and comfort in favor of training, practice, and self-improvement. It is through these disciplined actions that they cultivate the necessary skills and qualities to rise above the rest.

A champion's path is not always linear; it is littered with twists and turns, unexpected challenges, and moments of doubt. Yet, it is precisely these adversities that forge an unbreakable spirit. Champions do not shy away from the difficulties they encounter on their journey; instead, they view them as opportunities for growth and self-discovery. They embrace hardships, recognizing them as catalysts for personal evolution, and harnessing them as a source of motivation to push even harder.

Victory is rooted in purpose and passion. It is achieved by pursuing something that holds profound meaning to the individual. When one is driven by a purpose greater than themselves, the battles become worthwhile, and setbacks become mere bumps in the road. The ultimate victory lies not just in accomplishing a goal but in realizing personal growth, making a positive impact, and leaving a lasting legacy.

The pursuit of victory requires mental fortitude. Champions understand that the mind is just as powerful as the body. They train not only their physical abilities but also their mental resilience. They develop tools to overcome self-doubt, fear, and distractions, fostering an unwavering focus on the path ahead. By mastering their inner world, they are better equipped to navigate the challenges of the outer world.

In the face of overwhelming odds, champions find a way. They do not succumb to external pressures or conform to societal expectations. They carve their own paths, setting audacious goals and believing that they are within their reach. They persist, even when everyone else doubts their capabilities, and they prove time and again that victory is not reserved for the chosen few, but for those who are willing to put in the work.

Victory is not defined solely by trophies, medals, or accolades. It is the transformation that occurs within the individual. It is growth, resilience, and the unwavering belief in oneself. It is the ability to persevere in the face of adversity and to emerge stronger than before.

So, remember, victory is not something that can be handed to you. It is not a guarantee or a birthright. It is earned through hard work, determination, and a never-ending belief in your own abilities.

Embrace the challenges, face them head-on, and let them fuel your desire for victory. With the right mindset, unwavering commitment, and an unyielding passion, there is no obstacle that cannot be overcome and no victory that cannot be earned.

53

PLAY WITH HEART,
OR DON'T PLAY AT ALL

In the realm of champions, where dreams are forged and destinies are shaped, there exists an elusive quality that separates the great from the ordinary, the extraordinary from the mundane. It is the essence of playing with heart, an unwritten law that transcends the confines of the physical realm of sports and dwells within the depths of the human spirit.

Playing with heart is not a mere act of showcasing exceptional athletic prowess or mastering technical skills. It goes far deeper, tapping into the very core of one's being, where an unyielding passion resides, waiting to be unleashed. It is a journey into the depths of the soul, a seamless fusion of mind, body, and spirit, creating a synergy that propels individuals to extraordinary heights.

When one plays with heart, a palpable energy permeates every fiber of their being, electrifying their movements, infusing them with an intangible force. It is a profound connection, a sacred union between the player's consciousness and the cosmic energy that surrounds them. In this state, the player is no longer an individual with a limited physical form but a vessel for transcendence, channeling the collective dreams, hopes, and aspirations of all who witness their performance.

Playing with heart demands an unwavering commitment to the craft, an unrelenting dedication to the pursuit of self-improvement and excellence. It requires a deep understanding that success is not measured solely by victories but by the transformative journey one undertakes, continuously defying their own limitations. It necessitates embracing the demanding path of sacrifice, investing countless hours of laborious practice, honing one's skills, and refining their character, all for the sake of achieving greatness.

Yet, playing with heart is not a solitary endeavor. It is intertwined with the collective pursuit of a team, a collaboration of souls bound by a shared purpose. It is the realization that the strength of the individual is amplified exponentially when fused with the power of unity. Each player dons the team's jersey, carrying within it the weight of history, tradition, and the hopes of the community they represent. They become custodians of a legacy, embracing the responsibility to honor the past, inspire the present, and pave the way for the future generations to follow.

Playing with heart requires an unwavering belief in oneself, a potent elixir that fuels the fires of determination and resilience, enabling individuals to overcome the most daunting of obstacles. It is an audacious defiance of doubt and fear, as players dare to challenge the limits of their potential, unraveling the vast depths of their capabilities. This belief not only propels them forward but also permeates the collective consciousness of the team, instilling a sense of unwavering confidence that becomes the bedrock of their success.

The path of playing with heart is not without its trials. It humbles the players, for it is in the crucible of defeat where the seeds of growth are sown most profoundly. Failure becomes the catalyst for introspection, urging players to gaze deeply into the mirror of self-reflection, to confront their weaknesses, and unearth the untapped potential that lies dormant within. With each setback, a player learns to rise stronger, to embrace the lessons presented by adversity, and to forge an unwavering resolve to continue chasing their dreams.

True champions understand that playing with heart is not confined to the boundaries of a sports arena; it extends far beyond. It reveals the true essence of the human spirit, embodying the indomitable will that exists within every individual to rise, to overcome, and to leave an indelible mark on the world. It sparks inspiration in others, serving as a testament to the resilience and fortitude of the human condition, reminding us that within each of us lies a spark of greatness, waiting to be ignited.

As the clock ticks and the stakes grow higher, let us heed the call to play with heart, to summon the fire within, and embark on this profound journey of self-discovery and self-mastery. For in the realm of champions, where dreams are forged and destinies are shaped, it is those warriors who courageously play with heart that etch their names in the annals of history, becoming beacons of inspiration for generations to come.

54

EVERY SETBACK IS A SETUP FOR A COMEBACK

Life often throws us curveballs that test our resilience and challenge our aspirations. We face moments of failure, rejection, and disappointment that can leave us feeling disheartened and questioning our worth. But within these setbacks lies an opportunity for transformation and growth, if we choose to embrace it.

Setbacks are not roadblocks; they are the unexpected detours that redirect us toward our true path. They shatter our preconceived notions and force us to reconsider our approaches, ultimately guiding us toward a more authentic version of ourselves. Each setback we encounter becomes a vital chapter in the narrative of our lives, shaping our character and molding our destiny.

When faced with a setback, it is only natural to feel a whirlwind of emotions. Frustration, doubt, and uncertainty may consume us, leading us down a path of negativity and self-doubt. However, it is during these moments of darkness that we must summon our inner strength and resilience to rise above the challenges that lie before us.

Setbacks carry with them profound lessons that can alter the trajectory of our lives. They serve as powerful teachers, revealing our weaknesses and areas for improvement. They force us to confront our limitations head-on and prompt us to acquire new knowledge and skills. In the face of adversity, we unearth hidden wellsprings of determination, creativity, and perseverance that we may not have believed to exist within ourselves.

Moreover, setbacks push us out of our comfort zones. They test the boundaries of our courage and urge us to explore uncharted territories.

As we venture beyond the familiar, our resilience grows, and we discover untapped reservoirs of potential. Through battling adversity, we transform into a version of ourselves that is more resourceful, adaptable, and capable.

Setbacks instigate introspection, compelling us to question our goals, values, and inclinations. They offer an invaluable opportunity for self-reflection, enabling us to evaluate the congruity between our actions and our desires. In their wake, we may find newfound clarity and purpose, realigning our priorities and steering our lives toward a more meaningful direction. Setbacks serve as potent catalysts for self-discovery, guiding us toward an intrinsic understanding of who we are and what truly ignites our passions.

In the realm of sports, setbacks are a part and parcel of the journey to greatness. Athletes face injuries, losses, and failures that threaten to dampen their spirits. Yet the most exceptional athletes know that setbacks are merely temporary setbacks. They view these moments as opportunities to refine their skills, strengthen their resolve, and come back with even greater determination. By reframing setbacks as setups for a comeback, they embody the essence of true champions—individuals who perceive success not only as a victory but as a journey laden with growth, resilience, and perseverance.

Indeed, setbacks are an intricate thread woven into the fabric of our personal and professional lives. They present themselves as humbling reminders of our humanity and teach us to embrace failure as a gateway to improvement. Each setback fosters resilience, patience, and the unwavering belief that, regardless of the circumstances, we have the power to rise above and forge a new path.

It is paramount to remember that greatness seldom comes without the presence of setbacks. They act as transformative milestones, redirecting our course and strengthening our resolve. Our ability to navigate through setbacks with grace and tenacity showcases our character and defines our journey toward success. Embrace setbacks because they can lead to accomplishment, for within them lies the catalyst for our ultimate triumphs.

Therefore, when life hurls a setback your way, do not dwell on the disappointment or frustration it evokes. Instead, view it as an invitation for growth and resilience. Approach each setback as an opportunity to learn, adapt, and emerge even stronger. Remember that every setback is a setup for a comeback and that you possess within you the unwavering ability to rise above any challenge. Believe in yourself, stay steadfast in your pursuit, and let your remarkable comeback be a testament to your indomitable spirit and unwavering determination.

May your setbacks fortify you, may your resilience inspire others, and may your unwavering spirit illuminate the path toward your ultimate triumphs.

55

THERE IS NO SUBSTITUTE FOR HARD WORK

In this chapter, I want to delve deeper into the undeniable importance of hard work in achieving success. While it is something that we often hear and repeat, it is essential to truly understand the underlying principles and mindset that come with embracing hard work.

Hard work is the cornerstone of achievement in any field, whether it be writing, entrepreneurship, sports, or any other pursuit. It is the driving force that propels us forward, helping us overcome obstacles and reach our full potential.

At its core, hard work is about more than just putting in the hours; it is about investing yourself entirely in your work and continuously striving for improvement. It requires a mindset that understands the value of disciplined effort, consistent practice, and a willingness to go beyond what is expected.

In today's fast-paced and instant-gratification-oriented society, the concept of hard work sometimes gets overshadowed or even dismissed. We are often seduced by the allure of shortcuts, quick fixes, and hacks that promise immediate success. However, the truth is that there are no genuine substitutes for hard work.

Hard work is about developing a strong work ethic rooted in discipline and perseverance. It is the ability to commit to a task or goal wholeheartedly, even when faced with distractions or challenges. Discipline is the fuel that keeps us going, even on days when motivation feels out of reach. It requires us to prioritize our goals and make intentional choices that align with our aspirations.

But hard work isn't just about pushing through and ignoring everything else in life. It is about finding a balance, a rhythm that allows us to rest and rejuvenate while maintaining a focus on progress. It means understanding our limits and recognizing that taking care of our well-being ultimately enhances our ability to work hard and achieve our goals.

Hard work is not a solitary endeavor. Collaboration and seeking guidance from mentors and peers can greatly enhance our growth and development. Surrounding ourselves with like-minded individuals who share our dedication and work ethic can provide support, accountability, and valuable insights. It is through connections and the exchange of ideas that we can expand our horizons and accelerate our progress.

But what sets hard work apart is the presence of passion and purpose. When we are passionate about what we do, work feels less burdensome, and more like an energizing endeavor. Passion fuels our motivation and feeds our enthusiasm, making the journey towards success more enjoyable and fulfilling. And when we align our work with a sense of purpose – a higher meaning or a desire to create a positive impact – our efforts take on even greater significance.

It is crucial to set realistic goals along the path of hard work. While ambition is admirable, setting unattainable expectations can lead to frustration and burnout. By breaking big goals into smaller, achievable milestones, we create a roadmap that enables us to celebrate the small victories along the way. Recognizing and acknowledging our progress not only fuels further motivation but also reinforces our commitment to hard work.

Hard work is not just an old adage; it is the foundation of true achievement. It requires discipline, perseverance, passion, purpose, and a commitment to personal growth. Hard work is not about shortcuts or instant results; it is a continuous journey of improvement and excellence. By embracing hard work, we open doors to limitless possibilities and increase the likelihood of turning our dreams into a tangible reality.

56

THE THRILL OF VICTORY IS WORTH THE AGONY OF DEFEAT

The thrill of victory and the agony of defeat are not just confined to the world of sports. They resonate deeply in every aspect of life, whether it be the pursuit of personal goals, the creative process, or the challenges we face on a daily basis. As a coach, I have witnessed the ebb and flow of triumph and setback in my own journey, and it is through the prism of my experiences that I delve deeper into the complexity of this human condition.

The thrill of victory carries with it a sense of validation and accomplishment, but it is often fleeting. There is a surge of adrenaline that courses through our veins, a rush of euphoria that momentarily masks all the doubts and fears that plagued us along the way. It is a moment of pure exhilaration, as if we have conquered the world and defied all odds. The triumph itself becomes an anchor, a marker of success that can be shared and celebrated with loved ones, friends, and well-wishers. Yet, beneath this exultation lies a deeper truth – victory is not just about the outcome, but also the transformation that occurs within us as we strive to reach our goals. It is a testament to our resilience, perseverance, and unwavering belief in ourselves. It is a reminder that dreams can become reality and that the impossible can be achieved through dedication and hard work.

Even during this jubilation, there is a sense of impermanence. The thrill that once engulfed us begins to dwindle, leaving behind an insatiable hunger for the next challenge, the next conquest. We become restless, continually searching for the next peak to conquer, the next milestone to achieve. This pursuit of victory becomes a constant companion, driving us to push beyond our limits, to challenge ourselves anew, and to seek out new avenues for growth. The thrill of victory, therefore, becomes a catalyst for personal evolution, propelling us forward on our path of self-discovery.

And yet, the journey towards victory is not without its fair share of pain and disappointment. The agony of defeat, on the other hand, is a more profound and intimate experience. It is a stark reminder of our vulnerability, our limitations, and our imperfections. It strips away the façade of invincibility and exposes our raw emotions. The agony cuts deep, like a bitter wound that refuses to heal. It taunts us with feelings of self-doubt, whispers of inadequacy, and the temptation to give up. It is in these moments of darkness that we are truly tested – to find the strength to rise again, to learn from our mistakes, and to summon the courage to persevere.

The agony of defeat shakes us to the core, forcing us to confront our deepest fears and insecurities. It is a humbling experience that reminds us of our humanity, our fallibility, and the fact that success is not guaranteed. The feeling of defeat may linger, haunting our thoughts, casting shadows on our aspirations. Yet, it is in these moments of vulnerability that we are given an opportunity for introspection and growth. Each defeat becomes a crucible, a testing ground for our resilience and adaptability. It is through adversity that we learn our most valuable lessons, gaining insight into our strengths, weaknesses, and areas for improvement.

The agony of defeat propels us to analyze, reflect, and adapt, transforming the pain into a powerful force that propels us forward. It teaches us the true meaning of perseverance, reminding us that failure is not an endpoint but a steppingstone towards success. It teaches us humility and empathy, enabling us to empathize with the struggles of others and offer support in their times of defeat. It teaches us resilience, arming us with the determination to rise above adversity and pursue our dreams with renewed vigor.

The agony of defeat can manifest as self-doubt, imposter syndrome, and relentless questioning of one's creative abilities. But it is precisely these moments that push us to refine our craft, to dig deeper into the recesses of our imagination, and to emerge with words that resonate and touch the souls of others. The agony of defeat becomes a source of motivation, driving us to hone our skills, experiment with new ideas, and explore uncharted territories. It is in the face of rejection and defeat that we find the strength to persevere and capture the essence of our vision.

In life, the thrill of victory and the agony of defeat are intertwined, intricately woven in the tapestry of our experiences. They are the two sides of a coin, inseparable and indispensable. Without the agony of defeat, victory loses its luster, its intrinsic value diminished. It is through the ebb and flow of triumph and setback that we cultivate resilience, deepen our self-awareness, and find meaning in our endeavors.

As we embark on this journey, embrace both the thrill of victory and the agony of defeat. Celebrate our victories, no matter how small, and use them to move towards greater achievements. And let us not shy away from the pain of defeat, but rather view it as an opportunity for growth, learning, and self-discovery. In the vast canvas of life, the dance between the thrill of victory and the agony of defeat is what gives our stories depth, resonance, and ultimately, a chance for greatness.

57

BE FEARLESS IN THE PURSUIT OF
WHAT SETS YOUR SOUL ON FIRE

In life, there comes a time when the mundane routine no longer satisfies the yearnings of our hearts. We find ourselves craving something more, something that ignites a fire within us, calling us to step beyond the boundaries of our comfort zones. It is during these pivotal moments that our true character is revealed, and we have a choice to make: to go forth fearlessly or to succumb to the grip of our doubts and insecurities.

Fear, that insidious force that lurks within the depths of our souls, seeks to hold us back from venturing into uncharted territories. It whispers to us subconsciously, preying on our deepest fears and anxieties, casting a shadow on the dreams that stir our deepest passions. We find ourselves plagued by a litany of 'what if's' and 'but's', all the while feeling trapped within the confines of our own minds.

Yet, if we dare to confront these fears head-on, to acknowledge their existence without allowing them to consume us, we can break free from their suffocating grip. To be fearless is not to deny the existence of fear, but to accept it as a natural part of the journey towards self-discovery and growth. It is to recognize that fear is merely an illusion, a self-imposed limitation that stifles our potential.

To be fearless means adopting a mindset of resilience and embracing the unknown. It is to venture bravely into the realm of uncertainty, knowing that within the depths of uncertainty lies the opportunity for transformation. It is in the face of uncertainty that we are forced to delve deeper into ourselves, to draw upon strengths we never knew we possessed, and to unearth hidden reservoirs of courage.

When we step into the realm of the unknown, doors begin to open. We encounter new experiences, unfamiliar faces, and uncharted territories. We stumble, we fall, yet we pick ourselves up, again and again. This resilience in the face of adversity is the mark of the fearless soul. It is through these moments of struggle that we discover our true strength and resilience, often far greater than we ever imagined.

But the path to fearlessness is not without its hurdles. Society, with all its preconceived notions and expectations, often imposes its limitations upon us. It whispers in our ears, suggesting that we conform to the status quo, settle for mediocrity, and abandon our ambitions. It questions the feasibility of our dreams, scoffing at our audacity to dream big. The opinions of others can be a powerful force, capable of extinguishing the embers of our desires if we allow them to.

In the face of such skepticism and judgment, we must remember that our dreams belong to us alone. They are the echoes of our deepest desires, the manifestations of our unique gifts and passions. We must silence the external noise, find solace in our own convictions, and fiercely protect our dreams against the naysayers.

Being fearless is not just a label; it is a state of mind, a way of living. It requires us to cultivate a deep sense of self-belief, to trust in the process, and to surrender to the grander plan unfolding in our lives. It necessitates that we release our need for control, allowing the winds of destiny to carry us to new horizons.

In the quest for fearlessness, introspection becomes a cherished ally. We embark on a journey of self-discovery, peeling layer after layer, unraveling the depths of our being. We confront our deepest fears, exploring the origin of their existence, and in doing so, we unveil hidden strengths lying dormant within.

Facing our fears takes courage, but it is through this act that we recognize the immense power we wield. We come to understand that the fear we once considered our enemy can be harnessed as our ally. It serves as a beacon, illuminating the path toward growth and self-realization. By embracing our fears, we transcend our limitations, stepping into a space of infinite possibilities.

As we venture into the unknown, we encounter not only external challenges but also the inner battle against our self-doubt. The voices of uncertainty and inadequacy creep into our minds, tempting us to turn back or settle for less. But it is precisely in these moments that we must summon our inner strength, reminding ourselves of our divine potential and the unique gifts we possess. When we trust in our abilities and navigate through doubt, we unlock new levels of confidence, propelling us forward on our fearless journey.

Fearlessness necessitates resilience, for setbacks are inevitable on this path of growth and self-discovery. However, setbacks are not signs of failure; they are paths towards success. Each stumble and fall serve as a valuable lesson, teaching us resilience, adaptability, and the importance of perseverance. It is through these trials that we develop the fortitude to overcome any obstacle and emerge stronger than before.

Ultimately, fearlessness is a testament to the depth of our passion and the unwavering determination to pursue what sets our souls on fire. It is a commitment to our truth, a declaration that we will not be confined by the boundaries of societal norms and expectations. It is a vow to live authentically, with unyielding authenticity, unwavering resilience, and unbounded joy.

So, my dear reader, I implore you to embrace fearlessness as your guiding principle. Honor the call of your soul, for within its whispers lies the blueprint of your purpose. Embrace the unknown, confront your fears, and refuse to be confined by external judgments. For in the pursuit of what sets your soul on fire, you will come to know the depths of your being, and in doing so, you will set ablaze the world around you with your brilliance.

58

CHAMPIONS KEEP PLAYING UNTIL THEY GET IT RIGHT

In the world of champions, there is a relentless pursuit of perfection. They understand that success does not come easy; it requires dedication, perseverance, and countless hours of hard work. But what separates champions from the rest is their unwavering commitment to keep playing until they get it right.

Champions are not deterred by failure or setbacks. They embrace them as opportunities for growth and learning. Every defeat is seen as a journey towards success. They understand that there is no shortcut to greatness and that true champions are forged in the fires of adversity.

Failure is not viewed as an outcome for champions, but rather a temporary setback. They maintain a growth mindset, using setbacks as valuable feedback to improve their performance. Champions embrace a process-oriented approach where their focus is not solely on outcomes but on continuous progress and personal growth. They analyze their mistakes, seeking to understand the root causes and make necessary adjustments. Mistakes are not indicators of weakness for champions, but rather opportunities to refine their skills and strategies.

When faced with challenges, champions display extraordinary resilience and mental fortitude. They cultivate a strong belief in their abilities and the capacity to overcome obstacles. They channel their energy into finding solutions and pushing through the barriers that lie in their path. Champions embrace the discomfort of failure and use it as a catalyst for personal transformation.

Champions understand that success is not linear. It is a journey filled with peaks and valleys. They have a long-term perspective and are willing to endure short-term setbacks for long-term gains. This requires patience and perseverance, as they know that progress often comes in small increments. They do not expect instant gratification but are willing to put in the consistent effort required to achieve meaningful results.

One defining quality of champions is their relentless work ethic. They understand that talent alone is not enough; it must be coupled with hard work and disciplined practice. They are willing to go the extra mile, putting in the necessary hours of training, even when nobody is watching. Champions understand that greatness is not a one-time achievement but a continuous pursuit that requires ongoing commitment.

Champions also recognize the power of feedback and seek out mentors, coaches, and advisors who can provide constructive criticism. They are open to learning and value the perspectives of others. They leverage their network and actively seek out opportunities to learn from those who have already achieved what they aspire towards. Taking personal responsibility for their growth and development, champions actively seek out knowledge and strive to become lifelong learners.

Beyond their journey, champions inspire and uplift those around them. They become beacons of motivation, leading by example and encouraging others to strive for greatness. They understand the importance of a positive support system and surround themselves with like-minded individuals who share their commitment to excellence. Champions extend their impact beyond their success, contributing to the growth of those around them and fostering a culture of excellence.

In summary, being a champion is not just about winning trophies or accolades. It is about embodying a mindset and a way of life. It is about recognizing that success is not guaranteed but earned through unwavering dedication, continuous improvement, and a relentless pursuit of perfection. Champions understand that the journey towards greatness is an ongoing process that requires self-reflection, resilience, and the willingness to adapt. So, keep playing until you get it right, for champions are not born; they are made through their unwavering determination to never settle for anything less than excellence.

59

YOUR SUCCESS IS DETERMINED BY YOUR DAILY CHOICES

In life, success is not a result of a single grand gesture or a stroke of luck. It is a culmination of the choices we make every single day. Your success is not dependent on one big decision or one extraordinary action; it is shaped by the small but significant choices you make consistently.

Each day presents us with countless opportunities to make choices that align with our goals, aspirations, and values. It is in these choices that we find the power to shape our lives and create the future we desire. These choices may seem insignificant at first glance, but they hold within them the potential to transform our lives in profound ways.

The choices we make when we wake up in the morning, for instance, can set the tone for the entire day. Choosing to rise early and start the day with purpose can create a sense of momentum and productivity that carries us forward. It allows us to seize the day and tackle our tasks and goals with enthusiasm. On the other hand, hitting the snooze button repeatedly and rushing through our morning routine can leave us feeling stressed, rushed, and unprepared to take on the challenges that come our way.

Choosing to prioritize self-care is essential in maintaining our well-being on all levels – physical, mental, and emotional. Whether it means carving out dedicated time for exercise, meditation, or simply taking a few moments to enjoy a quiet cup of tea, these choices contribute to our overall health and happiness. Self-care choices may seem small in the grand scheme of things, but they have a profound impact on our ability to show up as our best selves and make progress toward our goals.

Throughout the day, we encounter a myriad of choices, from mundane tasks to significant decisions. Small choices, like choosing a wholesome snack instead of indulging in junk food or focusing on a single task instead of multitasking may seem inconsequential at the moment. However, these choices accumulate, aligning with our desired outcome of personal and professional success.

Even more significant choices, such as choosing to step out of our comfort zone or taking risks, can have a transformative effect on our lives. These choices require courage and a willingness to embrace uncertainty, but they often lead to growth and new opportunities. By choosing to confront our fears and take calculated risks, we expand our horizons and open doors to experiences we may have never imagined.

Success is not solely about the choices we make in our external actions and behaviors; it is also deeply intertwined with our internal choices—the way we think and the mindset we adopt. Choosing a positive and growth-oriented mindset can make a world of difference in how we approach challenges and setbacks. It means consciously deciding to see failure as an opportunity for growth and self-improvement, believing in our abilities and potential, and viewing obstacles as pathways toward our aspirations rather than barriers.

Developing a growth mindset is an ongoing process that requires self-reflection and introspection. It involves being aware of our thoughts and consciously choosing to reframe negativity into positivity and limitations into possibilities. Through the power of our choices, we can shift our mindset from one of fixed beliefs and limitations to embracing the limitless potential within us. It is about consistently choosing thoughts and beliefs that support and inspire us, even in the face of adversity.

It is essential to recognize that success is not an overnight phenomenon; it is built upon the foundations of daily choices. It is about making the right choices, even when they are not the easiest or most convenient. It is about resisting the temptation to take shortcuts or settle for mediocrity. It requires the discipline and determination to consistently make choices that align with our goals, aspirations, and values.

During moments of fatigue, doubt, or a lack of motivation, it becomes even more crucial to remember that success is not achieved by one grand gesture but by the daily progress we make. It is a journey marked by small but purposeful steps forward. Each day grants us an opportunity to make choices that bring us closer to our desired outcome.

As you navigate the winding path toward success, take a moment to reflect on the choices you make daily. Embrace a mindset of growth, discipline, and resilience. Make choices that align with your goals, aspirations, and values. Seek progress, not perfection. Above all, believe in yourself and the power of your daily choices to lead you to success.

60

WINNERS FIND A WAY, LOSERS FIND EXCUSES

In the vast tapestry of life, where the threads of destiny are woven by the choices we make and the actions we take, the contrast between winners and losers persists, as complex and awe-inspiring as the countless stories that form the annals of human history. In delving deeper into this enigmatic realm, we must unravel the intricacies that underlie the journey of champions and those who fall short, understanding that beneath the surface lies a myriad of factors that shape and define their paths.

To truly comprehend the essence of winners, we must first grasp the essence of adversity. For it is through adversity that the mettle of a champion is forged, chiseled from the ordeal of challenges that test their resolve. The world of winners is not one of smooth sailing through tranquil waters; instead, it is a tempestuous sea where storms of doubt and uncertainty rage fiercely. Winners inherently understand that success rarely comes by chance or luck; it must be earned through strenuous effort, unwavering dedication, and a refusal to succumb to the allure of complacency.

Winners possess an unwavering belief in their faculties, recognizing that their talents, abilities, and potential serve as the foundation upon which greatness is built. Yet, they are also acutely aware that mere potential is an empty vessel without the vessel of action. It is through their relentless pursuit of self-improvement, constant refinement, and an insatiable hunger for knowledge that they transform latent potential into tangible accomplishments. They seek out mentors, study the lives of those who have succeeded before them, and relentlessly seek feedback and critique, recognizing that growth is both an individual and collective endeavor.

The road to victory is paved with both victory and defeat. Winners understand that every setback, and every detour on the path to success is an opportunity for growth and learning. They view failure not as a condemnation, but as an essential element towards progress. The lessons gleaned from their missteps become the building blocks of their success, allowing them to recalibrate their strategies, adapt to changing circumstances, and emerge stronger, wiser, and more resilient from the crucible of defeat.

But it is not solely their unwavering determination that sets winners apart; it is the unyielding sense of responsibility they assume for their destiny. Winners understand that they are the architects of their lives, endowed with the power to shape their destiny through the choices they make. They do not seek solace in the realm of excuses but rather embrace accountability as the guiding principle that propels them forward. They take ownership of their shortcomings, acknowledge their flaws and weaknesses, and strive to transcend them, recognizing that true success lies not only in their accomplishments but in the continuous evolution of their character.

Behind every victory, there lies a symphony of effort, sacrifice, and resilience. Winners possess an unparalleled work ethic, and a steadfast commitment to their craft that transcends the mere pursuit of extrinsic rewards. They willingly endure the solitary hours, the sleepless nights, and the countless sacrifices demanded by their ambition. They understand that success is not an entitlement, nor a guarantee; it is a product of their unswerving dedication, perseverance, and the countless hours of honing their skills in pursuit of excellence.

In stark contrast, those who falter in their quest for greatness are propelled by a contrasting mindset, one that often finds solace in the embrace of excuses. They are plagued by self-doubt, cloaked in the fear of failure, and are predisposed to attribute their lack of achievement to external circumstances. These individuals, often captivated by the allure of the comfort zone, seek refuge in a realm devoid of challenges, opting for the path of least resistance rather than taking the risks necessary for growth.

Losers navigate the treacherous waters of life without the compass of self-belief. They surrender to the alluring whispers of self-doubt, allowing their aspirations to be drowned amidst a sea of negativity and self-sabotage. They are apprehensive about venturing beyond their perceived limitations, shackled by the chains of fear, and unwilling to confront the discomfort and uncertainty that accompanies personal growth. They perceive each setback as insurmountable while failing to recognize the inherent potential within them to rise above adversity.

As we embark upon the exploration of human resilience, we must heed the lessons imparted by the tales of winners and losers. To become a champion in our own lives, we must cultivate the unshakeable belief that success is not a destination but a journey with challenges, setbacks, and triumphs. We must embrace adversity as an essential catalyst for growth, understanding that the path to victory is littered with temporary defeats. Above all, we must assume the mantle of responsibility for our destiny. It is through the choices we make and the actions we take that we carve our place in the annals of greatness.

As you embark upon your narrative of triumph, remember that winners find a way, while losers only find excuses. Embrace the challenges that lie before you, for they are the crucible in which greatness is forged. Embrace accountability for your destiny. You hold within you the power to shape your future. Above all, embrace the unwavering belief that victory is not a distant dream but an achievable reality awaiting its champion.

61

DON'T STOP WHEN YOU'RE TIRED

STOP WHEN YOUR DONE

In the realm of champions, where dreams transform into tangible realities and ordinary individuals transcend their limitations exists a profound and deeply rooted truth - the power of persistence. It is the unwavering commitment to press forward, even when faced with the daunting strains of exhaustion, which sets apart those who achieve greatness from the rest.

For champions, the notion of giving up is unfathomable. They comprehend that genuine success is not nurtured out of convenience or when circumstances align effortlessly in their favor. Rather, it blossoms from the consistent and unwavering efforts they devote, regardless of how fatigued their bodies become or how loud that inner voice pleads for respite.

With each relentless pursuit of their ambitions, champions encounter moments of physical and mental exhaustion. Weary muscles and aching limbs continually remind them of the demanding nature of their chosen path. The allure of rest grows increasingly tempting as the body yearns for relief, urging them to surrender to the comforting embrace of idleness. But in those seemingly insurmountable moments of fatigue, champions draw upon an untapped reservoir of strength within themselves. They delve into the depths of their being, summoning a wellspring of fortitude previously unknown, for it is at the precipice of exhaustion that they unearth their true potential.

In these grueling interludes, when muscles ache and minds falter, champions are faced with a choice. They choose resilience. They choose adaptability. They choose to thrive amidst adversity. Embracing discomfort, they recognize that it is through these trials that they experience the most profound growth. While ordinary individuals perceive fatigue as a dead-end, champions perceive it as but another hurdle to surmount in their relentless pursuit of success.

It is crucial to acknowledge that weariness does not equate to failure; it underlines the toil and dedication poured into their craft. Fatigue serves as a gentle tap on the shoulder, reminding champions of the vastness of their ambitions and the extraordinary effort required to attain them. So, when exhaustion arrives, champions welcome it with open arms, recognizing it as a testament to their unyielding pursuit of greatness.

Even in the face of such tremendous fatigue, champions refuse to allow weariness to extinguish the fire that burns within their souls. They steadfastly refuse to let their dreams fade away, lost in discomfort and weariness. Instead, they harness their resilience, finding solace in knowing that it is in these moments of profound exhaustion that they surpass their own perceived limitations.

The journey of a champion encapsulates the belief that limits are meant to be pushed, boundaries meant to be shattered, and new horizons meant to be explored. With each stride taken on this laborious path, champions accumulate an unwavering reserve of stamina and strength, fortified by their sheer determination.

Therefore, my fellow champions, engrave this truth within your hearts: Do not halt when plagued by weariness; halt only when you have reached the culmination of your aspirations. Embrace the weariness as a testament to your tenacious dedication. It is within the depths of exhaustion that you ascend to dazzling heights of greatness. Push through the barriers, step beyond what appears impossible, and let your energy propel you toward the realization of your dreams. Your unwavering commitment to persist, even when the odds are stacked against you, will not only define your character but also lead you to the pinnacle of success.

Stay resolute, keep forging ahead, and unleash your unrelenting spirit in the pursuit of your dreams. May fatigue become an ally, propelling you towards uncharted territories, and ultimately guiding you to a finish line that signifies not just an end, but a new, breath-taking beginning. Remember, my fellow champions, you do not halt when you are tired; you halt only when you have wholeheartedly accomplished your journey.

62

THE ONLY FAILURE IS THE FAILURE TO TRY

In life, we are often faced with challenges and opportunities that require us to step out of our comfort zones and take a leap of faith. It is in these moments that we have a choice to make: are we going to let fear hold us back, or are we going to embrace the unknown and give it our best shot?

The truth is failure is inevitable. We are all bound to stumble and make mistakes along the way. But the real failure lies in not even trying. When we let fear of failure or uncertainty paralyze us, we deny ourselves the opportunity to grow, learn, and achieve our true potential.

Fear, although often seen as a negative emotion, serves a purpose. It is our mind's way of protecting us from potential harm or disappointment. But in many cases, fear is simply a projection of what might happen, fueled by our own insecurities and doubts. We tend to exaggerate the consequences of failure and underestimate the possibilities for success.

Think about some of the greatest achievements in history. Whether it is inventors creating groundbreaking technologies, athletes breaking world records, or artists producing timeless masterpieces, they all share one common trait – they were not afraid to try. They embraced the possibility of failure and pursued their dreams with unwavering determination.

Thomas Edison, the inventor of the light bulb, famously said, "I have not failed. I've just found 10,000 ways that won't work." His relentless pursuit and refusal to give up in the face of repeated failures eventually led to one of mankind's most revolutionary inventions. Edison understood that failure was an integral part of the process, and each setback brought him closer to success.

Failure is not the end; it is merely a doorway on the path to success. Every failure brings with it invaluable lessons and experiences that shape us into better individuals. It is through failure that we learn resilience, perseverance, and the ability to adapt. Each setback provides an opportunity for growth and self-discovery.

But if we never take that first step and try, we will never know what we are truly capable of. We will never give ourselves the chance to achieve greatness and make a difference in the world. By letting fear control our actions, we limit ourselves and confine our potential.

So, let go of the fear of failure. Embrace the unknown and step out of your comfort zone. Take risks, pursue your passions, and give everything your best effort. Whether you succeed or fail, you will no longer be haunted by the question of what could have been.

Success, too, is not a singular destination but rather a continuous journey. It is not measured solely by achievements or accolades but by the lessons learned, the growth experienced, and the impact made along the way. Success lies in the effort, dedication, and resilience it takes to overcome challenges and rise above setbacks.

The journey of pursuing one's dreams is not always smooth sailing. There will be roadblocks, detours, and moments of doubt. However, each obstacle presents an opportunity for personal growth and learning. It is through facing adversity that we discover our strength, uncover our true potential, and build resilience.

Failure does not define us but rather teaches us valuable lessons. It humbles us to acknowledge our weaknesses, encourages us to analyze our mistakes, and empowers us to make necessary improvements. Only through failure can we truly appreciate the sweet taste of success when we finally achieve our goals.

As a writer, I understand the importance of taking risks and embracing failure in the creative process. Every sentence I write is an opportunity to explore new ideas, challenge conventions, and express myself on a deeper level. It is through the act of writing that I too confront my fears and doubts, knowing that failure is simply a step in the process of growth and improvement.

Moreover, as a writer, I have the privilege of sharing stories and I understand that my words have the power to inspire, uplift, and provoke thought. I strive to encourage others to step out of their comfort zones, pursue their passions, and forge their paths despite inevitable setbacks.

In a world obsessed with success and instant gratification, it is crucial to remind ourselves that failure is not something to be feared but rather embraced. It is a testament to our courage, resilience, and determination to keep trying, no matter the odds. By acknowledging and accepting the possibility of failure, we free ourselves from the paralyzing grip of fear and open doors to unimaginable possibilities.

Do not be afraid of failure, but rather fear the regret of not trying. Let us shift our perspective and see failure not as a defeat but as an opportunity for growth. Embrace the unknown, take risks, and strive for greatness. For in the end, it is not about the outcome but rather the journey of self-discovery, personal growth, and the satisfaction of knowing we gave it our all.

63

SUCCESS IS A STATE OF MIND

Success is a multifaceted concept that encompasses various aspects of life, guiding us on a journey of self-discovery, growth, and contribution. While external achievements and material possessions are often used as indicators of success, true fulfillment comes from a holistic approach that considers personal development, relationships, and overall well-being.

One important part of being successful is knowing what we want to do and what is important to us. This means understanding what we care about, what we are good at, and setting goals that match these things. When we do things that match who we are, it shows the real us and makes our lives feel really good and satisfying.

However, purpose alone is not enough to bring success into fruition. It requires consistent action and a relentless commitment to our goals. Successful individuals understand the importance of discipline and hard work. They set high standards for themselves and have the determination to overcome challenges and obstacles along the way. Through dedication and perseverance, they transform their dreams into reality.

In addition to hard work, success is fueled by continuous learning and self-improvement. Personal growth should be a lifelong pursuit, with each day presenting an opportunity to expand our knowledge, skills, and perspectives. Successful individuals embrace a growth mindset, seeking out new experiences, challenges, and perspectives. They actively seek feedback, continuously educate themselves, and adapt to the ever-changing world around them. This hunger for knowledge and growth propels them forward on their path to success.

Furthermore, success is profoundly influenced by the relationships we cultivate. Surrounding ourselves with positive, supportive, and inspiring individuals not only enhances our well-being but also provides a network of like-minded individuals who can offer guidance, support, and opportunities. Successful individuals understand the power of collaboration and teamwork, actively seeking out partnerships and connections that will amplify their impact. They engage in meaningful and authentic relationships, valuing the mutual growth and support that comes from connecting with others.

In the pursuit of success, it is vital to maintain a harmonious work-life balance. Although driven individuals may be tempted to believe that success demands constant hustle and sacrifice, neglecting our well-being and personal relationships can lead to burnout and overall dissatisfaction. Taking the time to rest, recharge, and nurture our relationships is essential for long-term success and sustainable happiness. It is the cultivation of a balanced life that ultimately allows us to thrive in all aspects and sustain the drive required to achieve our goals.

Moreover, true success is not solely measured by external achievements but by the impact we have on others and the legacy we leave behind. Making a positive difference in the lives of others, contributing to our communities, and leaving a lasting impact is the hallmark of true success. Successful individuals understand that their journey is not just about personal gains but about using their skills, resources, and influence to create a better world for future generations. They strive to make a meaningful difference by embracing social responsibility, practicing empathy, and championing causes that resonate with their values.

Ultimately, success is a deeply personal and subjective journey. It is not a destination but an ongoing process of self-discovery, growth, and contribution. By embracing a purpose-driven mindset, working diligently towards our goals, cultivating meaningful relationships, prioritizing well-being, and making a positive impact on others, we can embark on a fulfilling and transformative journey of success in all its dimensions.

64

YOU CAN'T SCORE
IF YOU DON'T TAKE THE SHOT

In life, we often hesitate to take risks and seize opportunities because of fear or uncertainty. We may worry about failure or rejection, and as a result, we hold ourselves back from reaching our true potential. However, this chapter reminds us of an important truth - if we never take a shot, we will never have a chance at success.

Every successful person has encountered failure and setbacks along their journey. They have faced rejections and made mistakes. But what sets them apart is their willingness to take a leap of faith and take action. They understand that without trying, they will never know what could have been.

Imagine a basketball player standing on the court, with the ball in their hands, but never taking a shot at the basket. No matter how skillful they are, no matter how much they practice, they will never score a point if they do not take the shot. It is the same in every aspect of life. Whether it is pursuing a dream career, starting a business, or asking someone out on a date, we have to take the shot to have a chance at success.

Taking a shot requires courage, determination, and a willingness to face the possibility of failure. However, it is through these experiences that we learn and grow. Even if we miss the first few shots, we can adjust our aim, refine our technique, and keep trying until we finally hit the target.

But there is more to taking shots than simply the act of trying. It is about embracing uncertainty and embracing the unknown. It is about acknowledging that life is full of risks and challenges and that growth only happens when we step outside our comfort zones.

Taking a shot requires a certain mindset, one that is open to resilience and adaptation. It means acknowledging that failure is not an endpoint but an opportunity for growth and improvement. It is through these failures and adversity that we become stronger and more capable individuals.

Moreover, taking shots is not just about personal growth. It also contributes to the greater human experience. Many groundbreaking discoveries and achievements are the result of individuals who took the risk to venture into the unknown. Think of inventors, artists, and explorers who pushed boundaries and redefined what was possible. Their contributions have shaped the world we live in today.

When we look at the world from this perspective, we realize that we not only owe it to ourselves but also to society to take shots. We owe it to future generations to push the boundaries of knowledge, to challenge the status quo, and to make a positive impact. By taking shots, we contribute to the fabric of human progress and inspire others to do the same.

But taking shots is not just about achieving personal success or contributing to society. It is also about self-discovery. When we gather the courage to take a shot, we learn more about ourselves and our abilities. We uncover hidden strengths and talents that may have remained dormant and untapped if we had not taken the chance. The journey itself becomes a transformational experience, where each step forward builds resilience, character, and wisdom.

Additionally, taking shots allows us to overcome the fear of failure. The fear of failure often immobilizes us, keeping us stagnant and trapped in our comfort zones. By embracing failure as a natural and necessary part of the learning process, we free ourselves from the constraints of fear. We come to understand that failure does not define us; it is merely an opportunity to refine our approach and grow.

Taking shots also cultivates the skill of adaptability. Life is unpredictable, and circumstances change. By being willing to take shots, we develop the agility to adjust our strategies and seize new opportunities. We become adept at navigating the ever-shifting landscape of life, knowing that even if we miss, there will always be another chance, another shot to take.

Furthermore, taking shots helps us build resilience. We learn to bounce back from setbacks, disappointments, and rejections. Each missed shot becomes a lesson in perseverance and determination. We develop the mental strength to rise again and the belief that with enough effort and resilience, we can eventually hit the target.

The path to success is paved with taking shots even if it means risking failure. Those who are willing to take chances and seize opportunities have a much higher chance of achieving their goals and fulfilling their potential. So, go out there, take those shots, and do not be afraid to soar. Remember that taking a shot goes beyond personal success; it is a contribution to the ever-evolving tapestry of human progress. Through taking shots, we embark on a journey of self-discovery, develop the ability to embrace failure, cultivate adaptability, and build resilience. So, gather your courage, step onto the court of life, and shoot for the stars.

65

CHAMPIONS NEVER SETTLE FOR MEDIOCRITY

In a world filled with average and ordinary, champions rise above the rest. They refuse to settle for mediocrity in any aspect of their lives. Whether it is on the playing field, in their careers, or in their personal relationships, champions strive for excellence.

Mediocrity is like a stagnant pool of water; it is comfortable and unchanging. But champions are like rivers, constantly flowing and evolving. They understand that settling for mediocrity is a disservice to their potential and a betrayal of their dreams.

Champions believe in the power of growth. They view challenges as opportunities to learn, adapt, and improve. They know that true success is not just about winning, but about the journey of growth and self-discovery that comes with pushing oneself beyond limits.

At the core of a champion's mindset is an unshakeable belief in their own abilities. They understand that self-confidence is not arrogance but a deep-rooted trust in their skills and potential. This belief propels them forward, even when faced with formidable obstacles. Champions embrace failure as a temporary setback, never allowing it to define their worth, but rather as a chance to analyze, adjust, and come back stronger.

Champions are relentless seekers of knowledge. They invest time and effort into mastering their craft. They study the greats who came before them, seeking inspiration and learning from their successes and failures. They constantly refine their skills, staying abreast of the latest trends and advancements in their field. They understand that true mastery requires a commitment to lifelong learning.

But champions also understand that success is not a solitary endeavor. They build strong networks and surround themselves with like-minded individuals who challenge and support them. They value collaboration and teamwork, recognizing that shared goals and collective efforts can propel them to greater heights. They celebrate the achievements of others, knowing that lifting others up creates a positive ripple effect in the pursuit of excellence.

To be a champion means embracing a work ethic that knows no bounds. Champions know that success is not handed to them on a silver platter; it is earned through dedication, perseverance, and sacrifice. They are willing to put in the extra hours, to make the necessary sacrifices, and to endure temporary discomfort for long-term success. They find joy and fulfillment in the process of pushing their limits, knowing that it is the journey itself that shapes them into champions.

Champions understand that they are not defined solely by their victories but by how they handle defeat and setbacks. They demonstrate resilience, bouncing back stronger and wiser. They possess an unwavering commitment to their goals, staying focused even during moments of doubt or uncertainty. They know that their dreams are worth fighting for, and they align their actions with their aspirations.

Beyond personal success, champions recognize their role as agents of change. They use their success and influence to make a positive difference in the world. They are aware of the responsibility that comes with their achievements and strive to leave a lasting impact. They advocate for causes they believe in, use their platform to support those in need, and inspire others to overcome their own challenges. They understand that true champions empower others, creating a ripple effect that elevates the collective human spirit.

In the end, being a champion is not just about personal glory but about a commitment to self-improvement and making the world a better place. It is about embracing challenges, believing in oneself, working diligently, and always striving for greatness. Champions understand that greatness lies not in being better than others, but in being better than who they were yesterday.

So, my friend, if you aspire to be a champion in your own right, remember that mediocrity has no place in a life well-lived. Embrace challenges as opportunities for growth, cultivate belief in your abilities, invest in lifelong learning, build meaningful connections, and commit to relentless effort. Be a champion not just in your achievements but in the impact you make on the world, for champions are not born; they are forged through perseverance, dedication, and an unwavering commitment to be the best version of themselves.

66

THE HARDER THE BATTLE, THE SWEETER THE VICTORY

In life, we are constantly faced with challenges and obstacles that test not only our resolve and determination but also our character and resilience. These battles come in various forms - personal, professional, emotional, and physical - and have the power to shape us into stronger, wiser individuals. While it can be tempting to seek an easy path, it is through these difficult moments that we truly discover the depths of our capabilities and unlock our true potential.

When we face difficult battles, it is natural to be engulfed by a wave of discouragement or doubt. The very nature of these challenges can be overwhelming, making us question whether we have what it takes to overcome them. We may find ourselves grappling with self-doubt, wondering if we possess the necessary skills or if our dreams are simply too lofty. These moments of uncertainty can be disheartening, but it is important to remember that even the most accomplished individuals have experienced and conquered their fair share of daunting battles.

These battles teach us the importance of resilience, perseverance, and unwavering belief in ourselves. In the face of adversity, we are forced to confront our fears, step outside our comfort zones, and adapt to ever-changing circumstances. It is during these battles that we grow the most, learning invaluable lessons about our strengths and weaknesses. We discover our capacity to endure, to persist, and to never give up.

The harder the battle, the more we come to appreciate the significance of perseverance. We learn that success is not an overnight phenomenon but a result of consistent effort and determination. It is the ability to weather storms, adapt to setbacks, and keep pushing forward that sets us apart from those who opt for an easier path. These difficult battles become a testament to our character, shaping our resilience and forging our path towards success.

The harder battles also teach us the importance of humility and self-reflection. They remind us that it is okay to make mistakes, encounter failures, and take a detour along the way. Each setback becomes an opportunity for introspection, allowing us to evaluate not only our strategies but also our mindset. We learn to seek guidance from those who have walked similar paths, understanding that collaboration and learning from the experiences of others can be instrumental in achieving victory. Through self-reflection, we develop a deeper understanding of our own values, motivations, and aspirations - guiding us towards a clearer vision of our goals.

When we face hard-fought battles and emerge victorious, the taste of triumph is unparalleled. It fills us with a sense of accomplishment, satisfaction, and pride - a testament to our unwavering determination and ability to rise above adversity. The sweetness of victory represents the culmination of our efforts and sacrifices. It is a reminder that we are not defined by our failures or setbacks but rather by our resilience and the power of the human spirit.

The harder battles, although daunting, have the potential to transform us in profound and extraordinary ways. They present us with an opportunity to grow, to discover our hidden strengths, and to become the best versions of ourselves. Embrace these battles, for they have the potential to shape our lives and lead us towards the true essence of victory. Let each victory be a flame that ignites new possibilities and serves as a constant reminder of our ability to overcome any battle that comes our way.

FINAL THOUGHTS
THE CHAMPION'S JOURNEY NEVER ENDS

As we reach the final pages of this book, I hope the message that has resonated is that the journey of the champion never truly ends. There is no definitive finish line, no moment of arrival when one can claim absolute victory and retire from the pursuit. The path of awakening and actualizing your inner brilliance is lifelong.

There will always be new obstacles to confront, fears to overcome, and opportunities for growth if you seek them. Champions understand this. They know that self-improvement and self-discovery are not finite goals but daily endeavors. Excellence is not a permanent state but an unwavering commitment to bettering oneself.

I hope you walk away from this book with a newfound belief in your abilities and a curiosity about your untapped potential. But do not let that spark of motivation burn out or be extinguished by adversity. Fan it daily through perseverance, dedicated effort, and a willingness to step outside your comfort zone.

Surround yourself with supportive individuals who see your strengths even when self-doubt clouds your self-perception. Learn from your mistakes and failures but do not be defined by them; they are merely a means to an end on your unique path. Keep your eyes trained on the horizon but do not overlook the beauty and opportunity of the present moment.

Your journey as a champion has many more miles yet to be written. Embrace both the sweat and the glory that lie ahead. I am honored to have accompanied you for this segment, helping awaken your inner brilliance and resilience. But your story continues, champion. So, march boldly forward, conquer new frontiers, and ignite the power within. This is only the beginning!

Don't miss out!

Visit the website below and you can sign up to receive emails whenever Odell Theadford publishes a new book. There's no charge and no obligation.

https://books2read.com/r/B-A-CPDZ-BSVXC

BOOKS 2 READ

Connecting independent readers to independent writers.

About the Author

Odell Theadford is an ordained minister, aspiring mystery writer, and author of self-development and personal growth books currently living in Fort Worth, Texas with his wife Dr. Marcia Theadford. Though Odell has been involved in ministry for over 35 years, spreading the gospel and transforming lives, he has recently pursued passions for both mystery writing and penning self-help books aimed at personal growth.

He is drawing on his decades of experience working with people from all walks of life. His time providing counseling and facilitating workshops has given him deep insight into human nature and motivation - invaluable knowledge for crafting an intriguing mystery as well as for writing about personal development.

He is dedicated to developing the complex characters and plot twists that exemplify the mystery genre, while also using his understanding of the human condition to write self-help books focused on empowering people, finding purpose, and achieving their potentials. He finds writing fiction and non-fiction to be creative outlets allowing him to explore new forms of storytelling.

Odell is devoted to honing his craft as an author of both mystery novels and personal growth books. He spends hours each day writing and revising his manuscripts, striving to perfect the pacing, clues, and revelations that keep mystery readers guessing, as well as refining the practical wisdom and guidance offered to readers of his self-help works. He brings the same passion and dedication for writing that made him an inspiring minister. Pick up one of his books today and discover transformative wisdom or an intriguing mystery.

Read more at https://odelltheadford.org/.